To Dear Dorothy,
You are so dear!, So Bright!,
Thank you for you!

Laurie Kanyer

The JOURNEY ♥ OF BECOMING A MOTHER

Laurie A. Kanyer

TOOLS FOR A NEW MOTHER'S
EMOTIONAL GROWTH & DEVELOPMENT

The Love and Logic
PRESS Inc.
Golden, Colorado

The Journey

of Becoming

a Mother

ISBN 0-944634-32-X

Library of Congress Cataloging-in-Publication Data
Kanyer, Laurie A., 1959-
    The journey of becoming a mother : tools for a new mother's
emotional growth and development / by Laurie A. Kanyer.
      p.   cm.
    Includes bibliographical references and index.
    ISBN 0-944634-32-X
    1. Mothers—Psychology. 2. Motherhood—Psychological aspects.
3. Self-help techniques.
HQ759.K32 1996
306.874'3—dc20   96-3339
                                         CIP

Text Editor: Adryan Russ
Cover & Text Designer: Bob Schram
Illustrator: Dianna Schmidt
Photographer: Elisabeth Pedemonte

Printed in the United States of America

What Is Success?

To laugh often and much;
To win the respect of intelligent people
and the respect of children;
To earn the appreciation of honest critics
and endure the betrayal of false friends;
To appreciate beauty;
To find the best in others;
To leave the world a better place whether by a healthy child,
a garden path or a redeemed social condition;
To know that even one life has breathed easier
because you have lived;
This is to have succeeded.

—RALPH WALDO EMERSON

The Journey
of Becoming
a Mother

DEDICATION

This book is for
Douglas Peter Kanyer

ACKNOWLEDGMENTS

Theological expert and poet, Father Jeremy Driscoll, once told me that there are no new ideas, just new reconfigurations of those ideas with a twist of the present. Given the number of sources of inspiration I want to acknowledge in presenting this book, I believe Father Driscoll is right.

The original focus for many of these people was entirely different from that of this book. I have translated their ideas to the childbearing year, because I believe deeply that families need these ideas—from the beginning. Jean Illsley Clarke once said that this book is a "healing/prevention book." I believe this is true. New families, or people about to become new families, don't have to wait until a baby is born. They can use the materials now.

There are dear friends and colleagues who worked hard to make this project possible. My own personal collection of friends—Karen Kershaw, Linda Linneweh, Rosanne Bacon, Suzanne Bacon and Karin Carlson—formed an unwavering vision for this project. Their continual interest helped me through every page.

Many thanks to Christina McCarthy and Gayle Harthcock who edited the original manuscript. Bless Lillian Cassidy, who proofread the prototype and Jim Wilkinson, who consulted on book design.

To Jean Illsley Clarke and Connie Dawson, your hours of guiding me through the developmental stages of book writing was an incredible gift. I hope to carry on the tradition of mentoring you have modeled for me. Know that the decision to continue writing was often based on your encouragement!

Early readers include Diane Patterson, Nancy Doyle, Ann Keepler, Jennifer Tate, Carole Gesme, Carol Barany, Gail Park Fast, Dianna Kallis, Susan Martin, Russ Osnes, Mary Paananen, Jean Illsley Clarke, Elizabeth Crary, Debby Morgan, Sandra Bardsley, Penny Simkin, Hope MacDonald and Ellen Rhoades. Bouquets to Monika Boos, my mothering soul mate. Many thanks to Anne Caffrey for her vision and to Kitty Harmon for pushing me to come up with a subtitle. Tim Carlson and Rick Wilkinson offered advice and confidence. To Traci Cozzocrea, Drew Lenore Betz, Jackie McPhee, Mary Hart and Carol Davis Perry, thank you for your ability to listen for hours.

Appreciation and admiration to Dianna Schmidt for her artwork and my dear sister, Elisabeth Pedemonte, for the lovely photos. Blessings to the many mothers who offered testimonies and suggestions—most notably Grace Clark, Amy Lindh, Jennifer Morgan, Christina McCarthy, Laurie Mooney, Sherilyn Knisley, Jami Olson, Shawn Campbell, Heidi Wells, Chris Walters, Ryan Ranger, Elizabeth McKiernan, Lynn Mueller and Nola Eades.

Thank you to the five people who encouraged me to write a book—Dr. Patrick J. Moriarty, for predicting the future, Kim Feitush, for keeping after me to write, Mary Sheedy Kurcinka, for the gift of your letter, Rick Linneweh, for the permission to proceed and Dennis Pedemonte, for seeing what others could not. Blessings to Linda Van Cleave, Shirley Sackmann, Judy Popp, Judi Salts and Darlene Montz for teaching me ways to make my journey of becoming a mother a healthy one.

To the miraculous strangers—Nancy Henry and Carol Core of Love and Logic Press, for initially seeing the possibilities, a definite debt to you two. To Adryan Russ, my editor, who made my words dance across the pages, bless you! To Lucy Valderhaug, Evelyn Devine and Fern Sorensen, my mother and grandmothers, thank you for the lessons in thriving and surviving!

Of the many people who helped support this book, most important is Doug Kanyer, my dear husband, who played the role of primary caregiver to our three children during the months I spent writing. And they thrived beautifully! It was Doug's undying love that helped me replant my own family garden. The experience of becoming a parent with him helped me use my childbearing journey as a catalyst for self-discovery.

Finally, to my three children—Elisabeth Ann Kanyer, Kirsten Ann Kanyer and Wyatt David Kanyer—each of you has offered me gifts that have enriched my life beyond anything I ever could have imagined.

❀ ❀ ❀

To the many authors and researchers whose inspirations, ideas and words can be found within, I truly thank you. I am blessed to have stumbled onto your ideas, to use them in my own personal mothering journey and to share them now to support the development of families in the childbearing year. It is with a grateful heart that I acknowledge you.

*The Journey
of Becoming
a Mother*

"There will be no garden without the gardener"

The Journey

of Becoming

a Mother

TABLE OF CONTENTS

Detours

Tools

Come When You Can

"There is nothing more thrilling in this world,
I think, than having a child that is yours,
and yet is mysteriously a stranger."
—AGATHA CHRISTIE

Since 1992, Memorial Hospital in Yakima, Washington, has offered "Come When You Can" sharing support groups for new mothers. Known as Discovery Group, they have been attended by over 500 women since their inception. *The Journey of Becoming a Mother* is composed of the real-life stories of these new mothers, what we've learned from one another in the group, and my experience as a facilitator working with them.

As you prepare to become a mother and tend to the new stranger about to enter your life, you have an exciting opportunity—to enhance your own growth and emotional development, a component of beginning motherhood often overlooked in the childbearing year. In so doing, you lay the foundation for building a healthy family—the single most important goal on your new path.

The supportive tools that were born in the Yakima Discovery Group to help you lay this foundation are now available for you to utilize on your personal journey. Whether you use this guide privately at home or in a group setting, my hope is that you will use the birth of your child as a catalyst for self-discovery.

The Path of the Childbearing Year

The childbearing year is traditionally defined as the nine-month period of time from conception to birth, but it is much more. The childbearing year actually lasts from the time a woman considers becoming pregnant until her baby starts to sleep through the night or weans from the bottle or breast (typically around age one).

There are five major components that together make up that year and culminate in a family. They are:

❀ **Pre-pregnancy:** This is the period of time when a couple begins to flirt with the idea of having a baby, cope with the disappointments of fertility issues or scramble around adjusting to an unexpected pregnancy.

❀ **Pregnancy:** This is the nine-month growth cycle of the child in the womb.

❀ **Birth:** Including all the powerful physical and emotional elements ranging from joy to heartache, this is the actual event in which the mysterious stranger enters your life.

❀ **Early Postpartum:** Beginning on the day of birth and ending six weeks later, this is a time when the family forms a clam-shell presence that envelops the mother and baby. The new mom, a recent creation herself, has "new eyes," and her world will never be the same.

❀ **Settling In—Deciding to Be:** During this term, the family unit is embraced; mother and father grieve the losses that come as a result of the birth.

It is my belief that this "year" is more typically two years. For those mothers who become pregnant again soon thereafter, the childbearing year may be extended or prolonged, multiplied by the eventual number of babies that come into a family.

There is nothing common about the phenomena that create another whole person or those that produce a new mother. No matter how a family-to-be focuses on pregnancy and birth, it rarely recognizes the effort it takes for a woman to accept pregnancy and survive postpartum.

Detours on the Garden Path

Every pregnant woman runs into detours that get in the way of her emotional development during the childbearing year. Such detours can impact a woman's emotional self on her journey. Sometimes they affect the way a woman views her childbearing experience for the rest of her life. For some women, a detour may affect self-esteem. A sampling of such detours might be:

❀ The pregnancy was unexpected
❀ The mother-to-be's mother was not supportive
❀ Labor contractions were far more intense than expected

The challenges presented by detours offer you opportunities for personal growth and development. They may challenge you to expand the dimensions of yourself. Like the deer eating the berry harvest, the aphids infesting a rose garden or the gopher that moves tulip bulbs as it tunnels through the ground, detours change the scenery in unexpected ways.

Gardeners experiencing detours have opportunities to learn new skills for adapting, like fence-building to keep the deer out, the use of ladybugs to reduce the aphid population and enjoyment of the process of "naturalization" as the tulips become an addition to the scenery of nature. By maneuvering through the detours you can enhance your self-esteem by learning new skills and finding ways to cope when things don't go as planned. You may find you become a stronger, more capable person by identifying, acknowledging and coping with detours.

We will address these detours and many others in this book. The study group of mothers who contributed to the development of this book report an average of three detours in their emotional development. What's most important to remember is that no matter how strongly you may be affected, most childbearing detours can be resolved.

Recycling the Legacy of Your Path

One of the beauties of becoming a mother is the privilege of reviewing the cycle of life. As a woman gives birth to a child, she has the opportunity to recycle the legacy she's been given. It is common for parents to reexperience their own childhood development prompted by the development of their children.

 The beauty of recycling is that new mothers can relive their own childlike stage of development while using adult skills to explore that stage.

A mother can heal the wounds from her past by receiving helpful care during her childbearing year. Research has proven that for women who believe they were not cared for well during their childhood, a positive childbearing experience can begin to help repair the pain of those childhood injuries. Positive experiences during this time of incredible change can turn a woman's life path toward health and security.

This gift from the universe offers another chance at emotional health. The mother who did not get the care she needed as a baby can get it now in motherhood. Studies show that the positive care a woman receives during childbearing can help her see herself as lovable, even if she may have been unable to see herself that way before. Her own childlike needs are met while she meets the needs of her own child.

All families have legacies buried in the soil of their individual histories. These legacies can affect the level of nurture available to the members of the new family.

The childbearing year offers hope to the family group as the new mother receives helpful care and examines previously dormant feelings and self-esteem decisions from her early childhood. A woman can choose to ratify or change the collection of decisions she made in her youth. For many of us, a genuine secret garden can be found only outside the terrain of our parents' fenced and mowed lawn.

Exploring the subtle issues of the childbearing year, resolving detours and understanding their importance can create a healthier path. This clearing process can help you behold the possibilities within you and shape your experiences in the landscape you now inhabit. The exercises, tools and activities in this book will help put them into an appropriate perspective for your life today—as a mother and as a woman.

How the World Looks from Where You're Standing

When we go to the garden nursery, we may choose daisies because in our life experience we came to believe that the daisy is the basic, crucial element in a garden. Our neighbor, down the road, may believe that the rose is the backbone of the garden, because she has her own "frame of reference."

Each of us carries our own individual frame of reference—a collection of experiences and beliefs that contributes to the way we look at the world. It is the multitude of beliefs, values and processes, including our cultural and spiritual backgrounds, that contribute to the way we function in this world. We hold our frame of reference dear because it validates what and how we think in our own personal corner of the world.

A frame of reference gives us a starting place from which to conduct the business of our lives. What's important to note, however, is that a frame of reference is expandable and pliable especially during the childbearing year. At any given time, we can find new and interesting ways to function while still holding on to some of our original values. As you wander through this book consider expanding your frame of reference, while holding on to those beliefs that fit your growing family.

Writing Your Personal Thoughts

Making the transitions we will be discussing can seem monumental when we're going through them. That's why journaling is encouraged in this book. It gives you the opportunity to explore and resolve your feelings on paper. Journaling can often help process your feelings and put you on a problem-solving path.

Remember, you are engaged in one of life's major mysteries: growing and giving birth to another human being. You are developing and will develop courageous abilities during your childbearing year. Journaling may be a key to understanding. Go ahead, continue on the path of exploration.

The book may be read sequentially, out of order, in spurts or while feeding your baby. It is your book. Mark on it, talk to it, circle ideas you really like or cross out ideas that are not supportive for you. You are a capable, thinking person. In your heart you know what will work best for you. However you choose to read it, it's here waiting for you. Just come when you can.

CHAPTER 1

The Support You Need

*"If mama ain't happy,
ain't nobody happy."*
—ANONYMOUS

L ife begins in the garden. My favorite Northwest landscape architect, Dennis Pedemonte, once planted 5,000 Dutch Golden Age tulips in September on the grounds of a hospital. Much to his surprise, the next spring the Golden Age tulips turned out to be a Creamy White Hybrid lily tulips instead.

Dennis was faced with a gardening detour—alternate plans. As a result, he was confronted with a number of possible responses—to pull out the Creamy Whites, to plant complementary colored plants nearby, or to let the hybrids remain. Most landscape architects will tell you that what seems possible on paper rarely comes forth in the garden, because nature rules.

In the same way, a new mother may experience unplanned events in her childbearing year that prove nature rules. Every new mother, like the landscape architect, must come to terms with the fact that what blooms may not be exactly what she planted.

An expectant mother may have to learn to adapt to any number of unexpected detours and find ways to make sense of her new role. That's why it's essential to learn, first of all, what you need to know about you to get through the childbearing year in an emotionally secure way.

Your Garden of Support

The support a mother receives from a team of caring adults helps her care for herself and her baby in a more loving way. It can also help her handle those unplanned detours that are simply part of living. There is much wonder in planting this garden called family life.

While birthing and planting are most certainly physical events, imagination and emotions play major roles in both miracles. Mothering is a process of nurturing and being nurtured. To be emotionally present for your baby, you need abundant amounts of emotional support. In order to do a good job of caring for your baby, you need to receive care for yourself.

 Your baby needs you to love yourself in order to internalize love for him- or herself.

I once heard about a woman who made a habit of visiting her parents on a regular basis. She loved being with them, because they were happy and obviously cared deeply for one another. When she saw them meeting one another's needs out of love for one another, she too felt loved and cared for.[1]

Your baby's development is greatly enhanced by experiencing care from parents who are emotionally full. While the postpartum period is a good time to start, even before your baby is born you will want to prepare the mind-set that will put you on this path. In families where children come first and parents come last, emotional support falls short.

Building Your Support System

Many an expectant woman approaches the birth of her baby with a great sense of hope and renewal. Whatever your dream, you deserve and need support during the childbearing year. The care you receive helps build a sturdy trellis so the garden-family can grow tall and healthy.

The "Doula"

In many cultures around the world, new mothers are nurtured and cared for by teams of supportive women called "doulas," whose primary job is to advocate for the new mother and support her in every way. These societies understand the keys to survival for the group. They realize that a childbearing woman must be guarded and cared for so that she can care for and nurture her young. Their wise rituals make a new mother feel supported, protected and loved.

Research was done in Guatemala by gathering large numbers of women together and dividing them into two groups. One group had a support person with them during the births of their babies; the other group had no support person. The results of the study were surprising. The researchers found that the women who had a support person:

- Experienced shorter labor
- Used less medication
- Perceived the birth experience as positive
- Bonded with their babies sooner
- Felt an overall personal sense of higher self-esteem

The conclusion was that women strongly benefit from being nurtured and cared for by significant individuals in their lives—

and so do their babies. There was improvement in the relationship between mother and baby when a doula was nearby. It makes sense that a person *dedicated* to support and defend the childbearing woman would create that difference.

Today the concept of a doula is catching on in Western society, as new mothers arrange for supportive care to maintain their health and well-being. Your doula could be a dear older friend, mother, mother-in-law, or sister. While some doulas are formally trained, others are not. The key characteristic of a good doula is her unwavering commitment to your needs and desires. (For more information you could see "My Tool Shed: Equipment to Enhance My Growth & Development" on page 13 for ways to find a significant support person. A sample contract you can make for care and nurture can be found on page 14).

The Father in Your Baby's Life

For a number of decades, there has been a growing trend to encourage fathers of babies to be a key support person in the childbearing process. Many positive benefits have resulted—one of which is that men seem to be more connected with the baby and the mother. This wonderful happenstance is more likely to ensure a positive family unit. The father's acceptance and appreciation of the childbearing process contributes to a new mother's positive emotional adjustment.

When a man loves the mother of the baby, accepts her in her new role, identifies with her, works with her on issues of change and commits to being a source of financial as well as emotional support, the family unit has an even greater chance of survival. Working together, the family unit has its best chance of coping with detours—those turns, in the childbearing road, away from the positive experiences of this new role.

This is a time of significant life change for the baby's father, too. He also is becoming someone new—a dad. The pressure to support his partner may usurp his own needs for support and learning. A new father may also experience grief in the dramatic changes fatherhood brings to his life.

> **Many men neglect their own needs for support in an effort to be strong and to support their wives; others don't know how to; and still others have never given themselves permission to do so.**

The male experience of childbearing is significantly different from that of the female, but he may also recycle, grieve, and experience the pressures of idealistic dreams that differ from the realities in his life. These issues can affect the quality and amount of support offered to the new mother.

What a new father can offer is unconditional support. That support will include taking care of himself, too. On page 11 you'll find a section called "My Toolshed: Equipment to Enhance My Growth & Development." There you will find a basic guide for the new father.

Communicating What You Need

You may have spent a large portion of your life caring for other people. Perhaps you've had a job with great responsibility, or have structured a well-planned life. Sometimes, caretakers need to shift roles and learn how to be cared for. Learning better ways to be cared for yourself can serve to make you a better caretaker.

The inventory provided in this chapter may offer a familiar checklist to those of you accustomed to putting things into a workable structure—those of you who have had to balance career requirements, stabilize home demands or juggle both career and home life.

The unfortunate part about becoming an adult is that as we grow older, most of us have learned to not ask for care. But, in truth, humans were not designed to read each other's minds. In order to receive the care you need, much like your baby, you will need to ask for what you need.

To survive in the world, human beings naturally adapt to whatever the world has to offer and come to believe that whatever is—is all there is. That may have made sense to you until now. By becoming a mother, you have a chance to reconsider the level of nurture that's been available and request more when you need it.

Go at your own pace as you get used to the bounty of nurture that is yours for the asking. Listen to the inner voice you've developed to cope with the world around you. Reassure the voice that you know the original garden plan included enough nurture for you to get your needs met. Let the voice know that you have an interest in doing that now.

You might wish to turn to page 15 where you will find "My Journal: Turning Over a New Leaf of Discovery" and "Your Nurture Checklist." Let the checklist be your guide as you start to plan for what you need. As you use it to nourish your emotional needs as a new mother, choose those that nourish you, like a flower being replenished by water. Keep in mind that the quality of nourishment you offer your baby is greatly enhanced by the care you receive.

Reading Your Emotional Barometer— Feelings of Sadness

It is natural for you to feel great sadness as you restructure your life to include your new role as a mother. Please know that your sadness is a normal response to the dramatic shift in your life. It is an emotional signal for you to give yourself permission to become totally involved in where you are as a person—a new mother.

Any time of change carries with it a vast display of natural emotions. There are losses, and there are also times of great joy and wonder.

Emotions are like an internal barometer.
They may indicate that there is some work to do.

The sadness you may feel may be your signal to grieve. Grief is the work that helps to make meaning out of life's losses. Or, sadness may be your signal to mourn forgone opportunities. Yet again, your sadness may be part of your acceptance of moving along the path of motherhood and parenting into an unknown world of twists and turns. Remember, your sadness may not be depression but rather a normal signal connected to the tremendous change in your life.

Consider reassuring yourself when experiencing any emotion. You might choose to say to yourself:

❀ "I see I am feeling _____ (fill in the blank)."
❀ "Oh, that's what's happening!"
❀ "I will use this feeling as a signal to pay attention to my needs."
❀ "I will use this feeling to help me get my needs met."
❀ "Maybe I need to call a friend or invite my sister to visit."

Taking action toward your grieving, rather than feeling lonely and deciding that there is nothing you can do about it, is accepting responsibility for going after what you need.

Along your mothering journey, your child's development will offer you ways to enhance the use of your emotional barometer. There is no greater change a woman goes through than becoming a mother. Because of the dramatic changes you may now be experiencing, your emotional barometer may register greater levels than ever before in your life. It may be normal for you during the child-bearing year to feel many strong emotions at once.

 Birthing a baby offers you the opportunity to expand the dimensions of your emotional world in ways you may never before have experienced.

A new mother who does not feel some deep level of emotion during this time of her life may be in denial. She may be actually cutting herself off from a natural human experience. This cutting off may rob her of life-enhancing abilities that will help her care for her new family. Remember these emotional swings are typical for someone who has experienced tremendous life changes. Often they are triggered by the change in her hormone level as well as the realization of the changes in her life path.

Did you know that 5% to 15% of all women in the Western world are affected by postpartum anxiety and mood disorders? With proper treatment, these disorders can be resolved. If you are concerned that you are experiencing postpartum depression, be sure to get medical and psychological care. You can find more specific information on postpartum disorders on page 212.

Your investment in yourself is an investment in the future. Take the time to determine what level of human support you want and need—then, go for it!

MY DETOUR:
Unexpected Developments on the Garden Path

DETOURS are issues or problems that come up during the childbearing year, often outside of our control. They are the unexpected circumstances that occur and can force us off our anticipated plan.

Consider these thoughts, which may help you identify any detour you may have experienced during your childbearing year:

❀ Consider which situations took you off what were your well-laid plans during your childbearing year.

❀ What were the circumstances?

❀ What key people were involved in the detour?

❀ How did you resolve the detour?

❀ How did you feel about yourself and others as a result?

❀ What did you learn?

❀ What new skills has this experience offered you?

❀ What conclusions did you come to about yourself as a result of the detour?

Remember while detours may take us away from what we'd rather have happen, often they provide opportunity for deeper lessons in life. Note any lessons you might have learned from your childbearing detours.

The importance of acknowledging a detour is to become aware of what affect they may have on your self-esteem. Women can form self-esteem decisions based on how they adapt to a detour. The goal of this book is for readers to become aware of all the ways they can interpret the events of a detour while gathering support and information along the way. If life is going to give us detours, we may as well benefit from them and use them as opportunities for growth!

MY TOOLSHED:
EQUIPMENT TO ENHANCE MY GROWTH & DEVELOPMENT

THIS TOOLSHED, which will appear at the end of every chapter, is meant to help you reframe your detours, renew yourself and get back on your garden path. It will provide "tools" for you to use—perhaps a thought to consider or an exercise to perform. You are a unique individual and can choose the tool that works best for you. Perhaps you'll select a road you haven't taken before. The choice is always yours.

I. What a New Father Can Offer

Your first tool is designed to help you request care from the father of your child. The following list is a basic support guide for him to offer you. You are invited to browse this list of helpful ideas. When you feel ready, think about showing it to him. You could make a time to go over it and share the ideas most important to you now:

❀ To coordinate household needs so that you can rest and heal from the birth.

❀ To understand that changes in your hormonal system may affect your emotions.

❀ To learn to acknowledge and understand what is happening during your postpartum expressions of emotions.

❀ To connect with the baby and accept his responsibility to develop a relationship with his child.

❀ To provide support for your united growing knowledge of how to care for this baby and to provide protection from others who might criticize.

❀ To accept that your sexual relationship will change for some time after the baby is born; and to understand that there are many ways to be intimate and that as time progresses, interest in intercourse will resume.

❀ To communicate on key issues affecting the new family group and feel connected to them.

❀ To be willing to admit the need for outside support and information, when needed, and have the courage to ask for it as well as receive it.

❀ To honor you as a woman and help you celebrate the miracle of the childbearing year.

MY TOOLSHED:
EQUIPMENT TO ENHANCE MY GROWTH & DEVELOPMENT

II. A Significant Support Person

CONNECTING WITH a significant support person (also known as a "doula," who can be female, male, young or old) provides mothering for *you*. If death, distance or strained relationship keeps you from having support from a family member, like your mother or sister, seek out another person to care for you. This person's role in your life is to nurture and care for your needs in a warm, wise, nonjudgmental way. You deserve to secure a relationship with someone who will provide you with unconditional attention for a few hours a day.

How to Connect with a Significant Support Person

❀ Approach a potential support person and let the person know exactly why you are asking for their support. Without knowledge of the desired relationship, the person will not be able to meet your needs. You can certainly have more than one significant support person in your life.

❀ If your first choice is not willing to help you in this way, ask someone else.

❀ Explain to your support person that the goal is to gather support for your emotional needs. Invite your support person to enter into a support contract with you—even if it's your own mother.

Support Contract

❀ I (support person's name) agree to provide (your name) with the following support items (list them).

❀ I (support person's name) agree to provide (your name) with the emotional support she needs as well as acknowledge what a good job she is doing as a new mother.

❀ I will ask (your name) to call another member of her support team when I am unavailable to help or at a place in my day where I need to take care of myself.

❀ I agree to honestly inform (your name) if she is contacting me at a bad time and agree to get back in touch with (your name) at a time when I can truly focus on her emotional needs.

❀ The duration of this agreement shall be from (insert date) to (insert date).

❀ Renegotiation of this contract can happen at any time during this arrangement in order to continue to supply helpful nurture.

❀ If at any time during the agreed-upon period the relationship is not helpful to either person, the contract can be renegotiated or ended.

_____   _____
Your signature   Support person's signature

MY JOURNAL:
TURNING OVER A NEW LEAF OF DISCOVERY

A T THE END of every chapter in this book you will find this garden patch meant for you to express your thoughts and feelings on paper, should you choose to do so. You can write, draw, doodle—anything that helps you acknowledge how important you are and how much you need the support you want during this extraordinary time.

A journal gives you the opportunity to write words you have not been able to speak—either to yourself or to others. Perhaps you will find it comforting to put them on paper. Or, writing them down may provide you with the motivation to speak them. Here's an activity to get you started.

Your Nurture Checklist

Whether you have a doula, a supportive father for your child or other family and friends to help you during this time, this checklist can help you determine and ask for what you might need.

Once you look over the following checklist, you may find it helpful to:

❀ Write down the items that appeal to you.
❀ Have your support team read the list.
❀ Determine the items that are most likely to be accomplished.
❀ Discuss with your team of caregivers what you believe you need.

You

❤ You deserve helpful care that is based on your personal preferences, from people who agree to care for you. You deserve people to look lovingly and adoringly at you, to marvel in the wonder that is you and to admire your individuality. You are worthy of having someone hold, stroke or pat you. You deserve to have people bring you warm, cozy blankets, a lovely cup of tea or a nourishing meal.

The House

❤ You deserve people to take care of the details of daily living, a comfortable nest—a home tidied by others so that you can settle into your new world of being a mother without doing housework.

❤ You have permission to grow at your own pace and take your time acclimating to your new surroundings. You deserve pretty things for taking care of yourself—sweet-smelling bath bubbles, softly scented sachets, new undergarments that fit or a lacy pillowcase on which to take needed naps. Nurturing items don't have to be expensive. A simple bouquet of wild flowers may be very nurturing.

Change and Your Body

❤ You deserve to be surrounded by inspirational symbols of change—such as flowers, postcards, pictures of butterflies.

❤ You deserve to invest in your physical well-being and to feed yourself healthy foods, get light exercise, keep yourself clean and tidy. You need time to adjust to your postpartum body and understanding that it may take time to melt weight from the pregnancy. You deserve to receive encouraging words about your body image. You can honor and respect your postpartum body.

❤ The time will come to schedule and resume your sexual life with your partner.

Feelings

❤ You have permission to feel all your feelings. Your emotions are normal. No two women express themselves emotionally in the same away. Know that you are unique and that you will express your feelings in your own way. You deserve:

• Help to identify the effects that postpartum hormones may have on your emotions and to ask questions about yourself, such as, "How am I doing?"

• Time to grieve the losses you experience by becoming a mother and credit for the many ways you accept the changes in your life.

• To feel the effect of creating another whole life with another whole destiny and to take the time you need to accept the level of responsibility that mothering carries with it.

Communication

❤ You are entitled to help in getting in touch with what is important to you. Your support team can learn to ask you: "What do you need?" "Anything else?" This team can offer heartfelt responses and use active listening skills—acknowledging what you've said and repeating it to make certain that you have been understood.

Advice

❤ Welcome suggestions only when they are nonjudgmental, such as, "I invite you to think about . . ." or "I have one suggestion if you are willing . . ." or "If you wish to use me as a resource, please call." You deserve protection from people who have their own programs and tell you what to do or tell you how to take care of your family.

Relaxation and Friends

❤ You have the right to rest when your baby rests; to relax and recuperate after the birth of your child. You have the right to time away from the baby and away from other members of your family, to recharge your batteries, worn down from the exertion of new mothering.

❤ You have permission to make new friends with other new mothers and to get together with them on a regular basis to share common experiences and wipe away the ill effects of isolation.

Baby Care

❤ You deserve:

• Someone to teach you how to take care of your baby and to patiently show you how to diaper, burp or swaddle your infant. Also, support that respects your personal timetable in learning the "technical" side of child-rearing.

• People who show confidence in your intuitive ability to anticipate your baby's needs and connect with your baby. Also, reassurance that you need not become an expert in baby care to do a good job. Mothering, like planting a flower, requires no technical knowledge—only a nurturing soul.

• Encouragement and permission to become totally absorbed in this little human, to ensure that he or she feels accepted.

CHAPTER 2

Honoring Who You Are

*"If our lives are to be healthy and our spirits are to grow,
we must be dedicated to the truth. For the truth is reality.
And the more we clearly see the reality of the world,
the better equipped we are to deal with the world."*
—M. SCOTT PECK, M.D., *THE ROAD LESS TRAVELED*

It is a human trait to measure ourselves against other people. We see a friend or family member perform a wonderful task or gesture and believe we ought to be able to do the same.

One of the new skills parenting offers you is a chance to see yourself as *you* are and to accept yourself for the lovable capable person *you* are. There has never been, nor will there ever be, another you. The way that you make it through and endure pregnancy is the best way you know how with the resources you have available. That's all any human being can do.

People are different. Each person has a preferred style of receiving and responding to messages. As a child, you may not have always been encouraged to honor the ways you naturally think and respond. Pregnancy offers you an opportunity to change all that.

As you explore the issues of your childbearing journey and begin to reframe, grieve, grow and develop through this experience, it is important to know as much as possible about your preferred style of interacting with the world around you. While marriage is a tremendous change, it does not rank in comparison to the impact of childbirth. Childbirth is the single most dramatic life change there is for everyone in the family group—the new mother, new father and siblings.

Who you are at this particular time—in addition to whatever else you may be—is woman on the verge of motherhood. There is no other time like this time. The path you've been walking takes an unforgettable turn. Your body changes, the elements that make up your body change, and so does your thinking.

What becomes most important is the care you take of yourself. Since you may not be accustomed to focusing on your "self," here are some suggestions to put you on that path. If you have not yet given birth, you can make a plan to include these essential ingredients.

Sleep and Relaxation—
Essential Elements in Caring for Yourself

Sleep is an essential element in your successful development as a mother. Your healthy journey will be significantly affected if you do not get your rest. Many adults feel that naps are a luxury, but during pregnancy and especially during postpartum, naps are a daily necessity—as much as food.

Each person requires a varied amount of sleep. A good way to measure your need for sleep is to consider the amount you needed before you became pregnant. Then add up the amount you are currently getting. Subtract current sleep patterns from your previous sleep patterns to determine how much you need to function in a healthy way.

Before baby was born (10 hours)
After baby's birth (6 hours)
I need to find ways to get this much more sleep (4 hours)

Sleep deprivation affects everything. If you avoided taking naps in the past because you woke up grumpy, know that when you reach postpartum, your needs will be different. Because your sleep is constantly interrupted all through the night in postpartum, you may not experience the same effect from napping that you had before your baby was born. You'll be grumpy if you *don't* take naps!

As you make plans for your life once the baby is born, put rest on your calendar. You need it to keep up with your rapid growth and development as well as the repair process of postpartum.

Discovering a Shady Vista for a New Mother's Relaxation

Relaxing is different for everyone, but most of the following will work for almost any woman who needs to kick back and take a load off her feet.

❁ Take a bath or wash your hair.
❁ Call a friend.
❁ Paint your nails or brush your teeth.
❁ Light candles.
❁ Polish some silver.
❁ Read a magazine.
❁ Sit on your front porch.
❁ Make a pot of tea.
❁ Give the room an aromatic treat: Take 2 cups of water, 4 tsp. cloves, cinnamon and a cut-up apple. Boil for 4 minutes and turn down to simmer.

The Planting Instructions for a Good Nap

❀ Announce aloud, "I'm going to take a nap," even if no other adult is around. This is your contract with yourself to really do it. Put out your "Please Don't Disturb" sign.

❀ Unplug the telephone, because even the sound of an answering machine can wake you up. Keep noise levels down. Use earplugs if little noises bother you.

❀ Wear anything you want, as long as it's fresh and clean. Get a comfy pillow.

❀ Darken the room and take a nap before you are too tired to sleep.

❀ Read something nice from a collection of short stories or browse a beautiful magazine. You may need to read to transition you from getting a cranky, tired baby to sleep, to becoming drowsy yourself.

❀ Take a nap any time the baby naps. Ignore the household mess and get into bed. It is vital for your sanity!

❀ Let your mind go blank. Visualize a boat going downstream carrying away your worries.

❀ Breathe deeply.

Time Away

During any time of tremendous change, a person needs time to adapt to the influences that are taking place. When a couple gets married, typically they take a honeymoon. The honeymoon offers time to get away from family and work influences and allows the people involved to get to know one another.

A Babymoon

In her book, *Breastfeeding for Working Mothers*, Dr. Marilyn Grams recommends a babymoon—time away from the hustle-bustle of daily living, and time to come to grips with a new stranger in the family. A babymoon can be taken by brand new mothers to get to know their babies, or by mothers of older babies to adjust to the pressures of new developmental stages, or it can be taken by mothers who work outside the home to connect with their babies over a weekend. The babymoon permits you to invest time in whatever relationship you choose.[1] (See "My Toolshed: Equipment to Enhance My Growth & Development" on page 33 for steps to planning a babymoon.)

A Vacation Close to Home

You can vacation in your own hometown and take the baby with you. The change of scenery may be renewing to your spirit. Many communities have wonderful, nurturing "bed and breakfast" inns. You can save travel time and boost the local economy. Eat in your room. Order Chinese take-out or pick up deli sandwiches. Eating in will save on "dress up time" so you can nestle in and get some rest.

Bring your VCR with you if you go to a place that does not provide one. Choose your favorite movies and cuddle up for a night of relaxation and entertainment. If you need to go someplace that has a different landscape, get in the car and drive!

A Real Getaway

❤ When your baby is older you may want some time alone without the baby. For the best possible getaway consider these thoughts:

• Travel during the "off" season, when crowds are not expected.

• If you go somewhere new, ask around and always consider the source of the recommendation.

• Remember, if you ask people whose idea of fun is great shopping and you want to simply cuddle up in front of a fireplace, you may not get the advice you need.

• Go to a familiar place. Then you won't have to worry about where you're going, what the service will be like and if your accommodations will be good.

• Speak to the innkeeper about your goals for the stay *before* making reservations. If you want to be left alone and not have to interact with other adults, ask how you can be accommodated. If you wish to enjoy adult conversation, inquire about social time.

Fun and Inexpensive Nurturing Activities

In today's world, fun can cost a lot of money. In fact, there are still plenty of things left to do that are fun, nurturing and inexpensive. Here are some examples:

Read Something Enjoyable
❀ Visit the library.
❀ Buy a children's book and read it to yourself.
❀ Buy a comic book.

Seek Entertainment
❀ Go to a matinee.
❀ Go to the bank and get a shiny penny.
❀ Buy some of your favorite cookies.

❀ Collect jokes and have your friends tape them on your answering machine.

Spend Time Outdoors
❀ Go fishing.
❀ Go for a long walk.
❀ Plant bulbs.
❀ Start a collection of pretty rocks.
❀ Sit in the sun.

Spend Time Indoors
❀ Putter in your house.
❀ Clip funny cartoons from the newspaper.
❀ Frame a picture of yourself as a child.
❀ Cuddle under a thick blanket.
❀ Get up a little early and shower in the quiet of a new day.
❀ Have someone give you a massage.
❀ Take a foot bath.
❀ Paint one wall your favorite color.
❀ Make a nurture corner full of your favorite things.
❀ Collect pictures of favorite rooms and keep them in a file to enjoy.

Go Almost-No-Money Shopping
❀ Go window shopping.
❀ Go on an imaginary five-minute shopping spree.
❀ Buy a pretty hanky.
❀ Buy some pretty panties.
❀ Buy a funny pair of socks.
❀ Purchase a new bookmark.
❀ Buy popsicles.
❀ Buy a scent ring to put on a lamp to make your home smell pretty.

Write, Draw, Create
- ❀ Write yourself a letter.
- ❀ Doodle.
- ❀ Start a family tree.
- ❀ Restore one of your favorite childhood toys.
- ❀ Frame a drawing you made as a child.
- ❀ Cover a shoe box with pretty paper for storing your favorite cards or other special mementos.

Enjoy Music You Love
- ❀ Buy a single of your favorite song and play it over and over.
- ❀ Get in the shower and sing at the top of your lungs.

Discovering the Precious Lovable Child You Are

*"The supreme happiness of life
is the conviction that we are loved."*
—Victor Hugo

Few people would argue with the fact that a newborn infant is lovable, yet many question the level of love they receive themselves and the levels they offer others. The Bible says, "Love thy neighbor as thyself." This quote means that we can only love our neighbor, husband, child or friend to the level we see ourselves as lovable.

To ensure high levels of love for a baby, nature offers a mysterious curiosity in the hearts of new mothers. Women, who months before the birth of their babies, had not considered their love level, may begin to experience a stirring curiosity about ways to get more love in their lives.

One way to discover the truth about your universal lovability is to take a personal inventory to determine the quality of "love-life" you've been leading. By looking at your "love-life," you can evaluate your positive sources of love and the sources that may be draining your "love-level" and plan for ways to get the love you need into your life.

The amount of love currently available to you may be based on the levels that people in your life receive from themselves. It may be that you have adapted to the current level because you don't feel deserving of more, or because no one is willing to consider this issue. You can receive from not only what is available, but you can also consider ways to ask for and receive more.

A Personal Love-Level Inventory

To renew your curiosity about your level, consider taking inventory to look at what's happening in your life, to consider your long-term dreams and get balance and perspective in your life.

> *"There never has been, nor will there ever be, another you.*
> *In the great plan of life you are destined*
> *to receive unconditional love."*
> —LAURIE A. KANYER

Step 1: Relish the time new motherhood offers and pause to reflect on the course of your life. While caring for your infant, during times of feeding or rocking, pause to consider your love levels and allow yourself time to dream about abundant love.

Step 2: Get in touch with early thoughts you held onto as a child.

Step 3: Answer the questions in the following chart, or write them down in a journal.

My Personal Inventory

WHAT'S HAPPENING NOW IN MY LIFE?

❀ What are the intimate relationships in my life? List each person
❀ Are they offering me unconditional love?
❀ Will they accept unconditional love for me?
❀ Do I have to be someone else to receive their love?
❀ How much energy is it taking to earn the amount of love that is offered?

WHAT I KNOW ABOUT WHO I REALLY AM

❀ Consider your early thoughts about your life path.
❀ List some dreams you had as a child related to the love in your adult life.
❀ As a child what did you think your adult life would be like?
❀ What have you given up to be on the path you are on now?
❀ How do you think you strayed from your dream path?
❀ What illusions from the past do you need to help you feel and act lovable?
❀ What elements in your life can help you to believe and act lovable?
❀ What childhood beliefs take you off your lovable path?
❀ What's currently going on that gets in the way of your true lovable path?

A PLAN FOR CHANGE

❀ I wish to keep these elements of love I am receiving (please list).
❀ I wish to trash these elements that keep me from getting the love I was born to receive (please list).
❀ The following individuals will help me gather more love and remind me that I am worthy of receiving this love (please list).
❀ The following are affirmations I need to hear to believe that I deserve love (please name them).

MY TOOLSHED:
EXERCISES TO ENHANCE MY GROWTH & DEVELOPMENT

❤ The Old-Message Voice Inside

You may be hearing a voice inside fretting because you are not doing everything you believe you should in order to be loved. Part of the gift of parenthood is to challenge old paths and build a new one that leads to the truth about your self-worth—that you are lovable because you are you and for no other reason. Your baby does not have to do anything but "be" to receive unconditional love. Neither do you.

"Self love . . . is not so vile as the sin of self-neglecting . . ."
—WILLIAM SHAKESPEARE

❤ The Illusion of Love and Appearance

As we grow up and adapt to life in this world, we may buy into the illusion that love levels are based on appearance. We may have become someone other than our true self in order to receive love and recognition in our world. The world of fashion and beauty products is a multimillion-dollar business that tries to get us to buy beauty products, fancy clothes and clothing worn by beautiful models in magazines. An unfortunate result is that we may have come to believe that only beautiful people deserve love.

Having a baby forces you to carefully consider this rule. How many of us can keep up with these illusions? Being up all night with a baby, struggling to get rest and attempting to maintain a working household may dip into your ability to look "lovable," as prescribed by the fashion world.

Motherhood offers women a chance to adjust their values connected with the illusion of beauty and lovability.

While we may hear an inner voice that says, "Get back in shape and do something with that hair," we also hear a voice that says, "Take your time. You are beautiful as you learn to care for yourself and your baby. I'm glad you are you."

What's Lovable?

❀ Think about how you appear to yourself in the morning, all ruffled from a night's sleep. This is the real you, and you are lovable just that way.

❀ Consider the way your baby appeared shortly after birth—squished, slimy, maybe even bloody. Ask yourself if this little, messy being was lovable.

MY TOOLSHED:
EQUIPMENT TO ENHANCE MY GROWTH & DEVELOPMENT

I. Plan a Babymoon [2]

❃ Schedule an ample amount of time—two weeks for new mothers and a weekend for mothers with older babies.

❃ Create privacy. Take the phone off the hook, put a "please don't disturb" sign out and pretend you are "away." Hold the babymoon in your bedroom. Stay in bed if that feels comforting. Snuggle up with the baby, fluff your pillows, nap and feed when you wish.

❃ Use the time to practice nursing, caring for your baby and communicating. You need to create your own way of functioning in your new role. Invite supportive people, if you choose. All others can come around later.

❃ Reduce your responsibility level. Let household chores go undone or plan for someone else to do them. Say no to social engagements or volunteer responsibilities. Don't cook, wash clothes, clean house or entertain guests. Use take-out and frozen food!

❃ If there are older children in the house, it's a good time for their father to invest in his relationship with them. If the children's father is not in the household, request help from other caring adults.

❃ Put all equipment you might need for half of the day in a basket by the bed. This will keep you from having to go to another room to change the baby. The tools include diapers, two changes of clothing, bottom wipes and the small necessities typically kept in a nursery. Have a garbage can nearby for soiled diapers. Empty it occasionally on your way to the rest room.

❀ Keep things simple. Use disposable diapers. Sleep in comfortable cotton T-shirts, eat simple foods and stay in bed so the entire house is not consumed with all the equipment needed to care for the baby.

❀ Get help from friends and family members for meals and grocery shopping. While your family members or friends are shopping for themselves they can pick up some items for you. Ask for their support. You'll be surprised how willing they are to help. It will make them feel part of the process!

MY TOOLSHED:
EQUIPMENT TO ENHANCE MY GROWTH & DEVELOPMENT

II. The Healing Fence

THERE WILL BE TIMES in your mothering journey when you need to explore and feel your feelings. This is a life-giving, healthy process. The Healing Fence is a method for experiencing your feelings without allowing yourself to be totally consumed by the process.

Steps to the Healing Fence

❀ Discuss the problem with your support person. Ask for the amount of time you might need each day to feel your feelings. Write the amount on a sheet of paper. For example: "I will limit myself to spending 15 minutes considering the problem and exploring my feelings."

❀ Arrange for someone to spend time with the baby, at your residence, while you consider your feelings. For example: "David, I'll need 15 minutes each day this week to be alone to find solutions for my problems. Will you watch the baby from 8:00 to 8:15 tonight and the next six nights?"

❀ Spend your healing time in a safe, comfortable space, while someone you trust cares for the baby.

❀ Explain out loud to the baby that you need time to explore your feelings. Reassure the baby that he/she did not cause them, that feelings just "are." Reassure him/her that he/she will be getting good care while you are expressing your feelings.

❀ In your mind's eye, imagine a white square picket fence. Make the circumference of the fence you visualize big enough for you to fit in comfortably. The pickets represent the minutes you contracted for, and the space inside the fence represents a safe boundary in which to explore your emotions.

❀ In your mind, put yourself inside the fence for the time you agreed to be there. Explore your feelings. Think about them. Write them down. Spend time with them. Cry, yell, curl up or simply rest quietly and let the stress of the day melt away. Call a friend, if you prefer.

❀ When your designated time at the Healing Fence is over, write down a decision you've made about any concern.

❀ Share with your support person what was happening during your Healing Fence time and what decisions you made while inside the comfortable boundaries of the fence. Your support person may then be better able to help you evaluate whether you need further support.

❀ Choose an affirmation that helps you to heal, supports your decisions and validates your feelings. You can look on page 145 for a list of affirmations you may find helpful. Have someone say your affirmation to you.

❀ When those strong feelings creep up again, you can go to the Healing Fence again for an agreed-upon period of time. It doesn't have to consume your entire day.

 A Word About Strong Feelings: If you find that you are preoccupied with a problem, you deserve to see a counselor, a clergy member or a therapist for support. Many communities have organizations that offer counseling on a sliding scale. Don't let finances be a roadblock, see page 213 for suggestions on finding a therapist.

MY TOOLSHED:
EQUIPMENT TO ENHANCE MY GROWTH & DEVELOPMENT

III. The Pop-Bead Tool

WHEN PEOPLE HAVE CONCERNS IN THEIR LIVES, it is not uncommon to associate elements, issues and people that in actuality may not have anything to do with the real core problem. Strong emotions can cloud our perception of the real problem and possibly take us away from the true issue. By using the Pop-Bead Tool, you can string together all the elements you believe are connected to your concern—then, consider them one by one and disconnect those that are not really involved.

Here's how the Pop-Bead Tool worked for Cheryl.

Cheryl's Birth Plan

Cheryl had a complicated labor and delivery. The physician used many necessary, but unplanned, medical procedures. Ironically, during her pregnancy, Cheryl had written a birth plan in which she had expressed a desire to have few, if any, medical procedures.

The medical procedures she received during her labor, which included a Caesarean section, were used to save the life of her infant. Nine months after the baby was born, Cheryl felt sure that the medications used had caused harm to her baby, even though he appeared healthy.

To get the connections straight and help her begin to problem-solve, she used pop-beads. She named each bead as a person or issue related to her feelings and then isolated the bead troubling her the most.

She added beads for each of the issues and people involved in her concern, including one for herself. She then attached a bead for the baby, one for the birth plan, another for the actual events of labor and a bead for her fear of the medicine. When she got them all together, she said, "Everything is okay with every bead except the birth plan—the blue bead." The birth plan represented all her prenatal expectations about how the labor would proceed.

Cheryl had designed a birth plan to communicate her wishes during labor with her support team. She had requested no medication because she has a sister with mental disabilities whom, deep down, Cheryl believes was the victim of labor medication. Cheryl feared that the medication she received in labor might similarly affect her son, Jeff.

There was no evidence that the medications had affected Jeff in a negative fashion. But, Cheryl was still carrying this fear nine months after his birth.

We isolated the birth plan as the real problem. It was unrealistic. She was measuring her competence as a mother and a woman against the birth plan she had designed. She needed to evaluate the birth plan and work through the labor she actually experienced.

She was able to get the connection straight between what actually happened and how the actual events saved her baby's life. Cheryl was able to look at her baby and acknowledge that her baby was healthy and beautiful.

The Pop-Bead Tool helped Cheryl evaluate her prenatal expectations, her birth plan and how appropriate they were.

Directions for Using the Pop-Bead Tool

Here's what you'll need to use the Pop-Bead Tool for your particular situation:

❀ Two boxes of Fisher Price™ Pop-Beads, available at stores everywhere.

❀ Choose one pop-bead to represent:
  • You. Choose your favorite shape and color.
  • Each person related to the problem.
  • Each issue related to the problem.

❀ Imagine the connection between the people and the issues as you pop the beads together. Talk through the problem, starting with yourself. Pop in the next bead to represent the next person or issue. Pop the beads that represent your support team closest to the bead that represents you.

❀ Consider whether the arrangement you've created is helpful. Decide if each pop bead really fits in the order you've attached it, or if each should be connected to the string at all. If you are not pleased with the arrangement, remove any bead that does not fit.

❀ Thoughtfully consider each bead and the problem. Once you have considered all the beads, take off any bead that does not seem to really fit the core problem. Eventually you may have only the beads representing the real elements connected to the problem. This will help you to get some support for the true problem.

The Pop-Bead Tool will help you restore good feelings toward people or issues that you've discovered were not involved in the concern.

CHAPTER 3

Cultivating Your Nurture Environment

"When each individual life adjusts back to the harmony of nature's design, a much needed cultural shift begins—to organize emotional sustenance and the satisfaction of needs."
—PAM LEVIN, CYCLES OF POWER

When working on detours you experience during the childbearing year, it is helpful to identify the environment in which you are most likely to get the most exploration and healing accomplished. Because we are all different, we all feel comfortable discussing and sharing the issues of our childbearing journeys in different ways. That's why it's helpful to design a support-network environment, whenever possible, that fits *you*.

A designed environment for support is one in which a person can regularly review her life as it relates to the childbearing journey. Based on your level of introversion or extraversion, you can create an environment that's most helpful to you.

For introverts, the most supportive environment may mean one individual in a specific comfortable location, who ponders by herself the issues of the childbearing journey. She may then choose to discuss them with one or two others. For extraverts, the best environment may be a group and a comfortable physical location where the group gathers.

Are You An Introvert or An Extravert?

One way to discover your style and make a plan to get support that complements your particular temperament is to determine whether you are more introvert or more extravert.

Introverts derive energy from being with only one or two special people. They prefer to reflect on their thoughts and ideas before sharing them with others. The way they refresh themselves is by spending time alone.

Extraverts draw their energy from other people. They like to talk with people, share ideas and experiences in order to feel at one with the world. In order to feel refreshed and rejuvenated, extraverts need to be with and talk to people.

Look closely at the following desires, thoughts and actions and identify which defines you best. Put a check mark next to the ones that seem to ring true. Which feel the most comfortable? What would be your first choice—not what you've been *taught* to choose—but the one that fits *who you are?*

You are an extravert if you . . .[1]

❀ feel comfortable initiating a conversation

❀ easily come up with immediate answers for questions, or solve a problem by talking through the solution with someone else

❀ enjoy inviting friends over on the weekend; invite a few friends for dinner and realize you've invited the neighborhood

❀ need and like to hear that others admire your work

❀ easily reveal personal things about yourself

❀ chastise yourself for talking too much and not listening

❀ are exhausted by "too much" time alone, or only with young children

❀ find joy and energy in sharing a new idea or experience with someone

❀ are the one who calls the baby-sitter

❀ like to talk with someone at the end of the day

You are an introvert if you . . .

❀ can't imagine wanting to invite a group over on Friday night

❀ read the newspaper or zone out in front of the television after a hard day

❀ share personal information only with those who are very close to you

❀ have a long-time friend who's exclaimed, "I never knew that about you."

❀ think before answering a question, or berate yourself for not sharing an answer you knew; and solve a problem yourself before ever talking about it with anyone else

❀ know extraverts who interpret your thinking pauses as ignorance

❀ can't imagine enjoying dinner with the whole neighborhood present and prefer dinner with the family or one special friend

❀ find yourself hiding in a back bedroom at large family gatherings

❀ get tired of telling extraverts what a wonderful job they're doing and how much you love and appreciate them

❀ will do anything, even clean the toilets, if someone else will call the baby- sitter

Count how many statements you agreed with in each group.

Your Score: _____ Introvert _____ Extravert

If you checked more extravert statements, your energy more heavily relies on outside sources. If you checked more introvert statements, most of your energy comes from within.

One is not better or worse than the other.
They are simply two ways of being.
All you have to do is honor which one you are.

Now that you're better acquainted with your way of looking at the world, consider it in planning your mothering journey. You can make plans for getting your needs met based on your preferred natural style of interacting with the people in your life. By creating a way to receive care in a method that matches your style, you maximize the effect of the care.

What Is Your Most Nurturing Environment?

The support you receive is most useful if it is given in a way that fits your personality temperament and you are aware of environment options that complement your individual style. It is advantageous, whenever possible, to design a support network environment that fits the individual, rather than expect the individual to fit into any mold that is available.

An environment for support is one in which there is a time and place to regularly talk about your life as it relates to the childbearing journey.

If you lean toward being an extravert, your chosen environment may be a group of people on the same path who gather regularly in a specific location. If you tend to be more introverted, your environment of choice may be a certain time of day or week in a certain place, by yourself, where you ponder the issues of your childbearing journey and then make plans to discuss them with one or two others.

Naturally it's helpful to identify the environment in which you are most likely to get the most exploration and healing accomplished. The best environment for exploration is one that we can totally create to our liking. We already know, however, that what we sow is not always what we reap. So, the second best environment is the substitute we will take if the preferred method is not available.

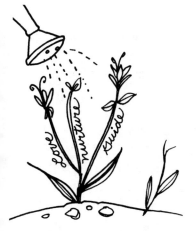

Think about the place or people you were with when you experienced memorable personal support that helped you resolve some of the detours of your day today, or some time recently. Did you call a friend? Did you wish you could talk with a large group of women? Were you in a special place?

With this recent experience in mind, continue to meander through the following environmental options. In each one, you'll find a definition of the environment and specific descriptors of the role it can play in providing support.

Your Environment Options

The suggestions that follow can help you determine the best environment possible for you. After determining the environment that suits you best, you can move ahead to resolve your detours and stay on the path of a healthy mother.

Environment Option 1—Extreme Introverts

Is this you? If you're an extreme introvert, having time to yourself is energy-enhancing. Time alone in your own personal space offers you optimal energy to resolve issues or detours where no one can interfere with your thought process or intrude upon your energy.

Environment Option 2—Mid-Range Introverts

While mid-range introverts derive energy from being alone, they also thrive on being part of small groups of people. Perhaps you have one or two close relationships or get together with small groups of friends from time to time. You maintain your well-being by balancing your introverted tendencies with occasional people gatherings.

Environment Option 3—Mid-Range Extraverts

Are you an extravert who gets your energy from being with people, but prefer not to be part of an ongoing group? Trying to work out your concerns alone doesn't work well for you. You need people to help you bounce ideas around, even if it's not on a regular basis. Whether small groups or large ones, you feed off the synergy that comes from being with others.

Environment Option 4—Extreme Extraverts

If you are an extreme extravert, you draw energy from being in a large group. You like large support groups and enjoy the process of helping them grow. The energy that comes from being with a lot of people is what drives you to come up with more ideas. You enjoy hearing what others are doing and sharing with them what you think.

If you wish to, peek ahead to page 52 for a tool for growing support based on your preferred style.

A Bouquet of Personal Compliments

Because so much of the information you save in your brain comes from words spoken to you, it's important to discover what method of receiving compliments, or strokes, means the most to you.

Researchers have found that each of us likes to hear compliments in a certain way. By discovering your favorite way, you can inform your support team and receive strokes designed and delivered especially to fit your individual style. Considering the weight of memories you are forming during your childbearing year, why not design compliments that mean the most to you—based on your personal preference? If a close friend asked that of you, wouldn't you want to give it to her?

Discovering Your Compliment Preference

Identify which way of hearing a compliment means the most to you. If you prefer a certain stroke in one special situation and a different stroke in another situation, please note that.

Ask yourself:

**Do I believe a stroke statement
(an affirmation or compliment) more when:**

❏ A. I say it to myself?
❏ B. I overhear people talking about me?
❏ C. The message is said directly to me?
❏ D. Someone tells me what others have said about me?

Check your preferred style of receiving a stroke

Someone with whom you are in a relationship wants to tell you he or she loves you.

Do you believe it more when that person:

❏ A. Takes the time to write you a note?
❏ B. Does some small chore or task, providing you a service?
❏ C. Visits your home and spends time with you?
❏ D. Tells you she or he loves you?
❏ E. Gives you some kind of gift or token?

Check your preferred style of receiving a message of love

By identifying your preferred style of receiving strokes, you will be able to tailor the kind of support that means the most to you. Go after it!

Carrie, The Extravert

To thrive, Carrie needs people. She also likes it when people report information to her about herself and she adores small, inexpensive gifts.

When her last baby was born, her friends threw a shower for *her*. She received simple pieces of inexpensive jewelry, picture frames, quote books and bath salts. She felt deeply loved, because she was able to receive nurturing in a way that meant the most to her.

It is vital to know your individual style as you learn new ways to ask for care. You deserve to have your needs met at this miraculous time, and it's more than okay to ask for this. By openly discussing your partiality toward certain ways of receiving love and affection, you will increase the likelihood of achieving your heart's desires.

As you read through this book, continue to consider your temperament style. You were born to be who you are. By learning about who you are and accepting and celebrating who that is, you can explore new motherhood in the healthiest possible environment.

REMEMBER:
It is your job to ask for and receive helpful support.
Therefore, it's essential to determine
what level of human support works best for you.

MY TOOLSHED:
EQUIPMENT TO ENHANCE MY GROWTH & DEVELOPMENT

Ask yourself:

> **1.** How does being an introvert or extravert affect me getting what I need?

> **2.** How do I feel when I lean more in one direction than the other?

> **3.** What are some actions I can take to help myself?

Getting What I Need as An Introvert or An Extravert

Introverts:

❀ Keep in mind that since your tendency may be to stay home and be solitary, you may need regular breaks away from your infant. While you enjoy being alone, too much isolation can have a negative effect while you're in postpartum. Constantly being around your baby may keep you from enhancing your personal development.

❀ Because isolation sometimes contributes to a feeling of being "the only one" with your concerns, you may tend not to seek out other people. You may want to form a close relationship with at least one other person who is parenting a similar-aged child. Then, you are assured that you are not the only person in the world with your particular issues.

Extraverts:

❀ Since your tendency is to get what you need from and with other people—often large groups of people—you will need to find an appropriate group. You may need to try more than one until you find the "right" one. Or, sometimes belonging to more than one will serve diverse needs.

❀ Many of us have schedules that keep us from getting together with a group, but we nevertheless need friends in our corner who support us. Put together your own group if you need to. Choose the people in your life you find most supportive and who you feel benefit you most.

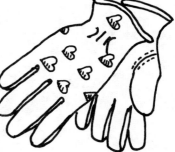

MY TOOLSHED:
EQUIPMENT TO ENHANCE MY GROWTH & DEVELOPMENT

I. A Breakdown for Introverts & Extraverts

Option 1: Extreme Introvert

DECIDE ON ONE PERSON you will talk to about the issue and recruit that person to check in with your progress on a regular basis. Form a close relationship with one *other* person—another mother who is parenting a similar-aged child. Discuss your journeys of becoming a mother with this woman.

Here are some wonderful small ways to treat yourself:

❀ Play some of your favorite music; make tea, in a teapot; sip it slowly.
❀ Meditate, pray or read from a spiritual book.
❀ Take a walk or just step outside; visit a friend or relative.
❀ Go to the grocery store or window shop at your favorite store.
❀ Look at beautiful objects. Talk with merchants or other shoppers.
❀ Find a book on star-gazing. At night, sit out and identify constellations.
❀ Go to a museum or art gallery.
❀ Attend a religious service. No matter what your religious belief—perhaps you have none—sitting in the midst of ritual, beautiful sculpture, candles and incense may be very healing.

> *"In solitude we give passionate attention to our lives,*
> *to our memories, the details around us."*
> —VIRGINIA WOOLF, *A ROOM OF ONE'S OWN*

Option 2: Mid-Range Introverts

A "MINI DISCOVERY GROUP" is a sharing support group of a few mothers who are parenting similar-aged children. Finding three or four other women with similar-aged children to meet on a regular basis can be very assuring. You can meet in each other's homes.

The primary role of the Mini Discovery Group is to reduce feelings of isolation. It's a place to share your feelings, celebrate your successes, generate suggestions for your concerns and find solutions for your problems. You can allow yourself to be heard and tell your mothering story to people who understand.

Here's a way to begin:

❀ Start the group with an outside stroller walk.
❀ Meet at a comfortable gathering place.
❀ Offer healthy snacks and a shared pot of tea.
❀ Provide some music dedicated to motherhood or inspired by children.
❀ Plan an opening exercise to welcome the group— a favorite poem.
❀ Sing a song together.
❀ Scent the room with an aroma everyone in the group likes.

"One of civilization's tasks is to find rituals which give human existence significance."
—JOHN BARRINGTON BAYLEE

Option 3: Mid-Range Extraverts

A Collection of Friends

A COLLECTION OF FRIENDS can provide the same level of support and intimacy as a discovery group or any organized group.

The key to making this work is good organization. Typically the collection of friends are individuals whose one common connection is: they know *you* very well. A group of five is recommended—people of different ages who have had varied life experiences—who understand why you are seeking their help. Part of their agreement may be to say "no" when they cannot help you. In those instances they can encourage you to contact another member of the collection who can:

❀ Provide you with affirmations, when you ask for them.
❀ Offer you suggestions when you actively ask for ideas.
❀ Not rush to solve your problems or pass judgment on you—just listen.
❀ Recommend someone you would enjoy visiting with.
❀ Leave positive messages/affirmations on your answering machine.
❀ Be an unlimited resource of affection.

"A friend is a gift you give yourself."
—AUTHOR UNKNOWN

Option 4: Extreme Extraverts

MANY OF US get energized in large groups consisting of more than 12 people. Perhaps you'll want to start or find a Discovery Group that is open to the entire community to serve the needs of any mother seeking support. (See Chapter 10 for more on Discovery Groups.)

Typically, the group is facilitated by the same person each time and mothers are encouraged to "come when they can" to the group, on a drop-in basis. For now, think about how helpful it is for you to be around other mothers. If you feel supported when in a larger group, consider investigating or starting a community discovery group of your own.

All excellent support groups and environments take into consideration the following elements.

❀ Soothing light
❀ Healthy, savory food
❀ Comfortable clothing
❀ Aromatic scents
❀ Warm, welcoming words

> *"I am not of that feather to shake off my friend*
> *when he must need me."*
> —WILLIAM SHAKESPEARE, *TIMON OF ATHENS*

CHAPTER 4

The Dreams, Realities & the Emotional Stepping-Stones of Pregnancy

"In early spring some seeds we sow,
and with what hope we watch them grow,
and waiting filled with such surprise,
we see each verdant shoot arise."
—AUTHOR UNKNOWN

As a new mother, you are in the process of forming memories. Considering that growing and birthing a baby takes nine months, it makes perfect sense that you'd want to connect the pieces of the whole story. Looking closely and recording the details of this miracle can help you do just that.[1]

The childbearing year offers an opportunity for joyous celebration, deeper emotional development and personal creativity for the whole family, especially the new mother.

While you celebrate the birth of your baby,
you can also celebrate your own birth—as a new mother.

Birth is designed to renew rather than complicate life. There are eight steps you'll want to consider as you review and celebrate this extraordinary experience. They are designed to make you feel secure, accepted and loved on this new journey.

Step 1: Seeking Safe Passage

Many expectant mothers begin their pregnancies with a strong desire to protect themselves and their unborn baby—which we call seeking safe passage. The concerns of most new mothers include nutrition, the effects of stress and competent medical care. A new mother seeks safe passage by securing a quality professional whom she can trust to give good care to herself and her baby. A pregnant woman needs to be with a medical/health care team with whom she feels secure—a team focused on everyone's well-being.

The pregnancy experience is full of double blessings—part of you is excited and overjoyed, while another may be worried and stressed. The importance of seeking a safe passage is to acknowledge that you are taking all the measures you know for the proper care of you and your baby.

As the pregnancy moves into the third trimester, you may find yourself preoccupied with *your* care as well as that of your baby. This is normal. Feelings of fright are normal. The night may be filled with frightening dreams. You may feel so excited that you can't wait to deliver the baby and at the same time be terrified about possible dangers you've heard associated with birth.

In the third trimester, there appears to be no separation between a new mother and her baby. What endangers one seems to endanger the other. Labor and delivery are perceived as double jeopardy to a new mother. The danger of not surviving, or of surviving but being somehow physically impaired, weighs heavily on her mind.

Exercises for Seeking Safe Passage

List things you did to seek a safe passage.

❀ Did you quit smoking?
❀ Did you quit drinking alcohol?
❀ Did you change your diet?

What issues got in the way of your plan for a safe passage?

❀ Did you suffer any illness during pregnancy?
❀ Did you work strenuous hours?
❀ Was it impossible to eat properly?

Have your caregivers provided you with what you need?

❀ Were you able to tell them what compliments you prefer?
❀ Did you tell them the support you need most?
❀ Did they understand what you asked for?

Write down some compliments/strokes for yourself for all the effort you put into securing a safe passage.

❀ ....
❀ ....
❀ ....

What are some issues you'd like to reframe (see glossary for definition) related to the plan for your safe passage?

❀ ....
❀ ....
❀ ....

What is important for your emotional development is how you felt about the care you actually received and the positive comments you receive for your efforts to ensure a safe entry into the world for your baby and a safe birthing experience for yourself.

Step 2: Accepting Yourself as a Pregnant Woman

Accepting the reality of the pregnancy on an emotional level is an important step for women. Acknowledging losses and opportunities is significant to your development. The acceptance circle begins with you and is supported by all the important people in your life. After becoming pregnant, many women experience vulnerability they have not felt since childhood. Some face feelings of loss of status as their earning power decreases or temporarily ends. Others feel unattractive or experience their physical abilities as compromised.

You may have had to face the loss of intimacy you enjoyed with your older child(ren). A new pregnancy may have forced you to move into a family model that calls for more children, work, and diapers. If you get most of your feelings of self-worth from the "doing" side of life—for all the tasks you accomplish—you may feel less worthy while you are pregnant.

The major task in accomplishing the job of acceptance is embracing the loss of control. Life as you have known it no longer exists. Remember you don't have to do this all alone, you can get support as you accept and process the changes. You gain new skills and become a deeper person during your childbearing experiences.

A Conversation with Myself— Considering Efforts of Acceptance

❀ What is becoming pregnant like for me?

....

....

❀ How does the pregnancy change the journey I am on?

....

....

❀ How does this pregnancy affect the quality of my life?

....

....

❀ Is this a planned pregnancy?
  How did the pregnancy change my life path?

....

....

❀ Will I grieve my losses?
  What do I consider to be the greatest loss?

....

....

❀ What are some feelings I've related to my pregnancy?

....

....

❀ What are some issues I'd like to reframe related to my pregnancy and the overall effect it has on the quality of my life?

....

....

Step 3: Securing the Support of the Baby's Father

*"Paternity is a career imposed on you
without any inquiry into your fitness."*
—ADLAI E. STEVENSON

Acceptance of the pregnancy on the part of your partner is critical. The father-to-be has a nine-month period to shift the basis for his relationship. A man becoming a father has a tall order ahead of him. The woman will change, the relationship will change, and life, while often enhanced by the birth of his baby, is never going to be the same.

Sometimes it's difficult to articulate what words you'd like your partner to provide you during this time. Chapter 1 has several suggestions about his support, but maybe what you want him to offer you is simply:

❀ **Joyous encouragement**
"Wow! I'm actually going to be a dad!"

❀ **Supportive comfort**
"You can count on me to be there for you."

❀ **Confident reassurance**
"It'll be fine—you'll see."

❀ **A sense of creative wonder**
"We're making a miracle!"

❀ **Understanding and partnership**
"This baby is going to change our lives. But we're in this together and he or she will bring so much joy."

Use the following chart to help you gather your thoughts on the words that are important to you.

Exercises to Examine
Your Partner's Acceptance

❀ List the statements you remember him saying to you. Write your feelings about those words.

❀ Ask yourself how the responses you heard affected the quality of your relationship.

❀ Write what you hoped he would say.

❀ Visualize yourself talking to him about what he said, if needed, so you can restore good feelings about the pregnancy, the baby and your relationship.

❀ List other ways he showed his support and acceptance during the pregnancy.

Step 4: Developing Acceptance from the Baby's Grandparents

"If becoming a grandmother was only a matter of choice
I should advise every one of you straightaway to become one.
There is no fun for old people like it!"
—HANNAH WHITALL SMITH

Acceptance on the part of the extended family and other important individuals, such as grandparents, is another crucial step for the well-being of a woman. It is important for expectant grandparents to resolve the losses they feel and offer messages of acceptance.

Expectant grandparents often fail to affirm the pregnant woman as they contemplate what effects this birth will have on their own lives. For some, it is the loss of status as the pregnant woman becomes a mother, or competition for power in the family unit that creates resentment or feelings of loss. For others, a fear of the continuation of an abuse cycle or simply the thought of getting older makes it difficult to embrace the new mother with acceptance.

While pregnancy brings about loss, it also brings about celebration and joy. One of the beauties of parenting and grandparenting is the opportunity to renew the garden path. Grandparenting offers a time to fertilize and strengthen the vines of the plant. Much healing and renewal can take place as grandparents are offered another chance to experience the marvels of childhood.

New grandparents have the opportunity to care for their child, the newborn mother, again if she asks for care during pregnancy and postpartum. If the expectant woman is a daughter-in-law, the mother-in-law and father-in-law may be offered a chance to connect and offer her support in ways not possible until the pregnancy.

Expectant grandparents are given a chance to reexplore their own memories of the childbearing year and smooth any rough spots. They have the opportunity to not only provide acceptance to the new mother but to regather their own acceptance for being parents. This contributes to their own well-being as well as to the new mother's.

Exercises for Acceptance by Parents/Grandparents

❀ List significant things you would like your parents or in-laws to do to display acceptance.

❀ List any statements that get in the way of your feeling accepted by them as a pregnant woman.

❀ Will you receive the level of acceptance you had always imagined?

❀ What are some positive strokes or compliments you have heard related to your pregnancy?

❀ What are some issues you wish to reframe related to the acceptance of your pregnancy by your family?

Step 5: Ensuring the Support of Your Personal Community

Growing a family garden is no small enterprise. A lot of faith happens during pregnancy—belief in miracles yet to be seen. The thought that an entirely new person is growing inside you is often an amazing concept to accept. But the acceptance by yourself and by others of the pregnancy and child-bearing process is a primary emotional step.

When a community of supporters cheers you on, you are more readily able to come to grips with the idea of pregnancy.

Samantha's Teacher

Samantha was a young woman of 22 when she discovered her pregnancy. She was excited, but worried. Married for one year, she had just finished college. She wanted her family to be overjoyed for her—to bless her and the baby she was creating. Like many women, she desired acceptance from her support group.

Samantha was delighted when she got a note of congratulations from an old high school teacher. The note was a concrete affirmation for the new person she was becoming, almost like a rite of passage—from one adult to, now undeniably, another.

During her pregnancy Samantha reread the note frequently. Gestures such as this one helped her accept the pregnancy and showed her that others were celebrating too. She particularly enjoyed it when complete strangers would gladly hold doors open for her.

Gaining an employer's acceptance also adds to your self-esteem and ability to relax if you've been spending many hours on the job. Sometimes it's not possible to acquire that acceptance—an employer may find it stressful to do without an employee while she's on maternity leave. Others are supportive and caring.

While there are payoffs, there are also losses, such as a reduction in free time as you tend to the chores. Your world may be turned upside down. It is helpful to your emotional health and that of your family and baby to consider what having a baby means to your quality of life.

**You can decide to love the baby
and dislike what having a baby did to your world.**

People in your circle of life may also go through ultimate losses. They know, consciously or subconsciously, that you are becoming someone "new." This may change how they respond toward you. Remember: you are learning more and more who you are, and that's what counts.

Step 6: Deciding to Love Your Real Baby

There is an emotional concept that a mother-to-be sometimes conjures up to help her cope with the idea of becoming a mother. That concept is a "dream baby," which helps the mother-to-be handle fears of not achieving a safe passage or facing the fact that her world is about to change.

While it is a normal thing to conjure up, it is important for you to put away that dream and begin to acquaint yourself with your real baby—the intimate new stranger who is about to become the focus of your real life. Through this acceptance, you come to terms with the impending birth and make plans to develop into a mother.

The time it takes to grow the baby offers an expectant mother time to accept this reality. This step is vital to the quality of attachment you feel shortly after birth. Give yourself ample time to let your love grow for your new baby. Let the dream baby melt away as you become accustomed to the child you delivered.

 You may have accepted that you were pregnant, while not accepting that you were really going to have a real live baby. The two issues are different.

Because the circumstances of pregnancy are different in each family, every woman accepts the real baby in a unique way:

❀ Women who planned and anticipate the pregnancy may have a smoother time in accepting the reality of the baby.

❀ Women who are coping with an unplanned pregnancy may find it more challenging to accept the reality.

❀ Those who planned a pregnancy in order to increase the level of love in their relationships may find it hard to imagine a live baby. They may be imagining the coming of a play thing rather than another human being with needs.

❀ For women who never imagined having a baby, accepting pregnancy and a real child as an end product may be a challenge.

Because becoming a mother is a journey, acceptance of your baby as a real child can take time. If you do not accept the reality of your baby until the baby is born, it's okay. It does not mean that you will not achieve a healthy pregnancy. It's a process, for which you must be patient with yourself.

Step 7: Giving: A Time of Unconditional Love and Support

The giving of oneself to another as completely as a woman offers herself to her baby is one of life's greatest sacrifices. A woman surrenders her body-self, possibly with some hesitance, only to wave a white flag giving in to the pregnancy. On a basic level she needs to come to accept that it is out of her control.

Pregnancy is a magnificent act of giving, giving and more giving from every corner of the community, from the individual to the large group. The process of giving helps the pregnant woman's self-esteem as she experiences acceptance from the community. This receiving of tokens helps her give and keep giving to the baby. It also sends a reminder that she, too, must receive in order to have enough to give the baby.

When a woman is offered gifts of acceptance from her support team it helps her to offer the gift of herself to the baby. The most helpful gifts from supporters are gifts that are assertive, supportive and unconditional in nature. You can find more information on gifts on the Nurture Highway on page 73.

❀ Assertive care gifts are offerings for which the caregiver becomes actively, maybe physically, involved in doing things the mother is temporarily unable to do herself. It might look like the preparation of a feast in honor of the mother, or tending to the heavy work of her prized garden that she may not be able to do because she is in advanced pregnancy.

❀ Supportive care gifts include a card of congratulations,
a maternity outfit or items for the infant.

❀ Any gift that comes with no price tag is a gift of
unconditional care.

Step 8: Accepting Your Body Image

As a pregnant woman, you move between being uncomfortable
with the changes that occur out of your control and the excitement
you feel as you experience a growing baby inside you. Certainly the
circumstances surrounding the conception of the baby affect the
range of your feelings concerning your body, but other social issues
can come into play.

Americans are fascinated with a youthful body. For this reason,
when you are pregnant and your body changes, so may your self-
image. If your self-esteem is wrapped up in appearances, you may
struggle with the impending growth you will go through and not see
it in a positive light.

Accepting physical changes and losses is an emotional step to
work through as you offer yourself affirmations for the miracle you
are creating, while grieving the loss of your young woman's body.

Some women may feel a sense of embarrassment because their sexual activity is exposed to the world. This can pose a great dilemma for
women who are single or those who choose artificial insemination.

Some mothers struggle with the idea of the redefinition of the
purposes of their sexual organs. Sexuality is redefined as a mother
moves from seeing her vagina and breasts as ways of expressing herself sexually, to ways of delivering and feeding a baby.

Many women get stuck as they redefine beliefs about physical discomforts. It may be difficult to acknowledge the symptoms of pregnancy—nausea, heartburn, frequent urination—as normal, physical pregnancy functions, when in previous experiences, they were considered illness.

Learning to trust the body's ability to produce a healthy baby can also be a challenge, especially if there has been a history of previous miscarriages or premature birth.

For women who pride themselves on their ability to physically accomplish a lot or for those who are exceptionally athletic, the physical restriction and decrease in physical ability can be oppressive. It is expected that a "normal-weight" woman will gain an average of 28 to 32 pounds during pregnancy.

The expanding uterus stretches vital ligaments, placing pressure on the bladder and pushing the diaphragm and stomach closer to the lungs. The expanded breasts require greater support, while the increase in blood circulation places additional demands on the heart. Understandably, these changes will affect a woman's physical capabilities.

This is not to say that a woman cannot find physical comfort or continue athletic activities in pregnancy. But she must adjust the physical demands she requires of her pregnant body. Women who derive most of their strokes from their physical abilities may feel at a loss because of perceived or real limitations. They may have to force themselves to a personal redefinition of what's doable.

Remember:
It takes both the sun and the rain to make a rainbow.

Appreciating the Detours—
Marveling in Unexpected Opportunities

A Story:

You are taking a vacation to Italy. You have saved and been planning this vacation for years. The day arrives, you board the airplane and get ready to enjoy your cross-continental flight.

The food offered is good, the company is pleasant, yet the flight is taking longer than you thought it would. You decide to consult a flight attendant.

The flight attendant replies, "Oh my goodness, you must not have heard the announcement when we were taking off. You're right— a flight to Italy takes nine hours, and most often we fly on time. This flight, however, is going to Holland."

Crushed, you can barely breathe. You want to flee, but obviously cannot. You sink into your chair, red-faced and angry. How could this happen? The person next to you pats you on the shoulder. "There, there, Sweetie, it will be all right. You can vacation in Holland."

Once in Holland you see that it is quite different from the Italy you expected. You feel angrier and more disappointed. Your entire vacation—the trip of a lifetime—is ruined. A tour guide approaches you. "Welcome to Holland, do you have plans for the day?" She offers you a bouquet of multicolored tulips, and they smell wonderful.

Hungry, you say, "Is there someplace I can get a meal?"

You spend your entire vacation in Holland. You discover the beauties of the country, you discover the beauty within you. You find that you can adapt, remold your thinking and find ways to thrive in what originally appeared to be a tragedy. You get to know Holland, and you get to know more about you.

—AUTHOR UNKNOWN

MY TOOLSHED:
EQUIPMENT TO ENHANCE MY GROWTH & DEVELOPMENT

The Nurture Highway

THE NURTURE HIGHWAY[2] is one way for people to evaluate the care, acceptance and support they received. The positive lanes on the Nurture Highway are assertive care and supportive care, which involve working cooperatively as adults to care for your wellness. Assertive care may consist of physical assistance when needed. Supportive care consists of help you can accept or reject.

On this highway, abuse represents the harshest kind of care, ranging from painful physical strikes to painful verbal strikes. On the opposite end is neglect, which offers no care at all, ranging from absence of care to being "too busy," or ignoring pain. While abuse and neglect are at opposite ends of the chart, their effects are similar. Each style ignores the needs a person may have for care and support.

When examining the Nurture Highway on the journey to becoming a new mother, be aware of the following points:

❀ Each lane represents responses you can receive from your support team, including medical professionals, the father of the baby, your parents and extended family.

❀ Each of us responds to the care offered differently because we hear or see responses from our unique perspective. Therefore, your responses to the lanes may not match those of others.

❀ You may have received nurture from all the lanes on the highway from many sources during the childbearing period as well as throughout your life.

Jean Illsley Clarke and Connie Dawson describe *nurture* in these terms, *"Nurture is all the ways we give care to ourselves and others. Nurture helps us thrive and develop. We store nurture droplet by droplet and it is the basis for our self-esteem. Nurture provides humans with attention and contact they need in order to stay alive and live fully."*[3]

The care the new mother receives during her childbearing journey provides her with the contact and attention needed to stay alive, care for herself and live fully, so that she can care for her baby.

These are steps to using the Nurture Highway. Follow them and see what happens!

❀ **Step One**—Write down a situation in which you received care that was not helpful. Also write one down in which the care you received was helpful.

Example: I asked for medication. "When I asked for medication in labor the medical staff refused. The staff person said, 'Are you always so uptight? If you would just relax your pain wouldn't be so strong. Come now be a good girl and things will be just fine.'"
(*In the example above, you may have heard the statement from the medical person as sounding like "Conditional Care." The statement had global words like "always" and offers care only if you were a "good girl."*)

❀ **Step Two**—Read through each of the columns of care that are offered on the Nurture Highway (page 76) and determine which one describes the response you received. Decide for yourself where it fits on the highway.

❀ **Step Three**—Think about how you wish the care had been given.

Example of Assertive Care: The physician says, "I understand the pain is intense, but you are at a place in your labor where the use of pain medication will slow down the progress. I'll be right here with you and will breathe with you through as many contractions as long as you need me. I'll observe your body and remind you to release the parts of your body that appear to be tense."

Example of Supportive Care: The physician says, "The pain right now is intense. Remember your desire to use as little medication as possible. You can get over this hump and I will be here to cheer you on. You are not alone. All your support team is here and we care for you and can see how hard you're working. Do you still think you need medication right now?"

Consider what effect each kind of care may have on your emotional well-being.

❀ **Step Four**—Rewrite the care you got. State it in a way that would have been more supportive. Have someone read it to you and listen for the difference between the responses.

❀ **Step Five**—Evaluate the effect of the care you received. Think about your emotional self.

• Did you get positive feelings about the care you got?

• Consider how much value, negative or positive, these memories have for your emotional self.

• Consider your feelings about the nurture you received. Can you see any effect on your self-esteem as a mother?

If you determine that there is a negative effect, make additional plans to resolve the issue. You may choose to seek support from a therapist, a clergy member, a support group or a member of your support team.

Here are the lanes of the highway:

THE NURTURE HIGHWAY

ABUSE
Characteristics:
Abuse is related to assault on your body, or your emotions, or the body and emotions of your child, by physical or psychological invasion, or by direct or indirect messages that mean "don't be." Abuse negates your needs or the needs of your child. It can be considered harsh treatment.

People Who Experience Abuse
May Hear the Following Messages:
You don't count. Your needs don't count. You are not lovable. You don't deserve to exist. To get what you need, you must experience pain.

Common Responses of People
Who Experience Abuse:
Pain felt in your heart as well as the physical effect of the injury. Fear, terror, loneliness, despair, shame.

Decisions Often Made by People
Who Experience Abuse:
I am not powerful. I deserve to die or the reverse: I will live in spite of them. It's my fault, or the reverse: I'll blame everything on others. I'll be good or the reverse: I'll be bad. Big people or people in positions of authority get to abuse, or, I can abuse those smaller than me, or, I will never abuse. I won't feel or have needs. Love does not exist. I am alone, I keep emotional distance from and don't trust others. I blame or strike first.

CONDITIONAL CARE
Characteristics:
Adults who use conditional care use threats or conditions. Statements like, "I will take care of you only if you . . ." or "If you don't do . . . I will not continue to care for you." The care that is offered is based on the caregiver's needs and the expectations of the relationship, but does not take into consideration the needs of the other person.

People Who Experience Conditional Care
May Hear the Following Messages:
I matter, you don't. Your needs and feelings don't count. You can have care as long as you earn it. Don't believe you are lovable, you have to earn love.

Common Responses of People
Who Experience Conditional Care:
Fear, terror, anger, mistrust of own perceptions, shame, feelings of inadequacy.

Decisions Often Made by People
Who Experience Conditional Care:
I am what I do. I must strive to please. Big people or people in positions of authority get what they want. I can never do enough. I must be perfect. I don't deserve love. There is scarcity of love. I must be strong. Love obligates me and is costly. I don't trust. I do keep emotional distance, run away, or blame others.

ASSERTIVE CARE
Characteristics:
Assertive care is comforting and loving. It is given freely without any strings or expectation of being paid back. It is helpful to the person receiving it and is responsive to the person's needs. It can be thought of as loving intrusion during the childbearing year, as the person provides physical assistance or comfort. This kind of care can be assistance with housework to helping a woman on with her shoes. For some women it may be the first time in a long while that she has needed this kind of help. Up until the pregnancy, a woman may have been able to care for many of her needs, pregnancy may force her to need assistance. During labor the assertive care of the support team can be demonstrated by responding to the need for help by the mother to move around her surroundings or to physically assisting with the pushing stage or by providing pain medication when she asks for it. It is appropriate to the circumstances.

People Who Experience Assertive Care
May Hear the Following Messages:
I love you and you are lovable. You are important. Your needs are important. I care for you willingly.

Common Responses of People
Who Experience Assertive Care:
Feels comforted, accepted, important, satisfied, relieved, secure, safe, loved.

Decisions Often Made by People
Who Experience Assertive Care:
I am important. I deserve care. It's okay to ask for what I need. I belong here. I am loved. Others can be trusted and relied upon. I can know what I need. It's okay to be dependent at times.

Adapted from *Growing Up Again, Parenting Ourselves, Parenting Our Children*, by Jean Illsley Clarke and Connie Dawson, ©1989 by Jean Illsley Clarke and Connie Dawson. Adapted by permission of Hazelden Foundation, Center City, MN.

SUPPORTIVE CARE
Characteristics:
Nurturing supportive care offers help, comfort and love. It encourages the person to decide if they want to accept care or if they are capable of doing it for themselves. During pregnancy it reflects an attitude towards the pregnant woman as healthy and capable. It may cheer her on as she maneuvers through her development. During labor it respects the phases of labor, allowing the woman to steer the course, while encouraging her and staying near for support. In postpartum it instills confidence in her abilities to meet her own needs and learn to meet the needs of her infant. It offers options of care and does not rush in, disabling the woman's confidence in herself.

INDULGENCE
Characteristics:
Indulgence is a sticky kind of care and a patronizing kind of love. It promotes continued dependence on the caregiver and encourages people not to think for themselves as well as not to be responsible for self or others. During pregnancy indulgence could look like someone doing all the household tasks while you rest, even though you are capable of contributing. In labor it might be the use of medication to take away the pain, even though the laboring woman is feeling on top of the labor. In postpartum, it could look like someone taking complete care of the baby in order to give you time to rest, even though you did not ask for the help. The people who offer indulgence may very well have needs of their own that they are ignoring to take care of what they think you need.

NEGLECT
Characteristics:
Neglect is passive abuse. It is lack of attention emotionally or physically by a support person or a caregiver who is unavailable or who ignores the needs of the person asking for care. These support people and caregivers are "there, but not there." In pregnancy it can look like a physician who doesn't answer questions or makes the patient wait for hours in the waiting room without explanation. In labor it can look like the medical staff not answering the call button, or going about the room doing other tasks but not being aware of your condition. In postpartum it can look like no one is assisting in the tasks of the household or assuring that the mother and baby are provide for.

People Who Experience Supportive Care May Hear the Following Messages:
I love you. You are lovable. You are capable. I am willing to care for you. Ask for what you need. Your welfare is important to me. I am separate from you. I trust you to think and make judgements in your own best interest.

People Who Experience Indulgence May Hear the Following Messages:
Don't be who you are. Don't be capable. Don't grow up. My need to be needed is more important than your needs or your needs are more important than mine.

People Who Experience Neglect May Hear the Following Messages:
You are not important. Your needs are not important. You do not deserve to exist. Expect to suffer to get what you need. Be confused about reality.

Common Responses of People Who Experience Supportive Care:
A feeling of being cared for, challenged in reasonable ways, secure and trustworthy.

Common Responses of People Who Experience Indulgence:
A temporary feeling of comfort that may end up feeling like self-centeredness, then later on; helplessness, confusion, obligation, resentment, defensiveness, and shame.

Common Responses of People Who Experience Neglect:
Feelings of abandonment, fear, shame, rage and abject disappointment.

Decisions Often Made by People Who Experience Supportive Care:
I am loved. I can know what I need. I am capable. I can be powerful. I am not alone. It's okay to ask for help. I am both separate and connected as a person, a woman and a mother. I can decide when to be dependent and when to be independent.

Decisions Often Made by People Who Experience Indulgence:
I am not capable. I don't have to be competent. I don't have to know what I need, think, or feel. Other people are obligated to take care of me. I don't have to grow up. I must be loyal to my indulging caregiver or support person. To get my needs met, I manipulate or play a victim role. It's okay to be self-centered. Later on: be wary and don't trust.

Decisions Often Made by People Who Experience Neglect:
I don't really know who I am or what's right. I am not important or powerful. I die or survive alone. It isn't possible or safe to get close, to trust or to ask for help. I do not deserve help. What I do doesn't count if someone has to help me. Life is hard.

MY TOOLSHED:
Equipment to Enhance My Growth & Development

Adjustments

THINK BACK FOR A MOMENT on some of your new life experiences over the past years—going to a new school, moving to a new house, getting married or making any long-term commitment.

❀ Did you spend time imagining how those events would turn out before they actually happened?

❀ Were there events in your life that you refused to think about because the thought of them happening was too much to believe.

❀ "Denial" is an emotional tool people use to cope with changes they are not ready for. While denial can be dangerous when safety is ignored and people are put at risk, when it is used to cope with changes in life, like childbearing issues, denial can be helpful. Have you used it?

❀ Having a baby has been romanticized by the modern media. We all do the best we can with the resources available to us in the moment. Have you found being totally responsible for another human to be overwhelming?

If we can practice accepting our "self" first, we can move toward accepting the new baby. What matters is that you spend time accepting the pregnancy and your very real baby. Some women do this acceptance during their nine months of pregnancy; others do it later.

Remember:

❀ It is not appropriate to "blame" the baby for coming into your life. Sometimes people end up together beyond their intentions. You can evaluate and grieve the changes in your life, but you do not have permission to imply that the baby caused the events.

❀ When you discuss the effect having a baby has had on your life, you must find a way to discuss it away from your baby. Infants deserve to have caregivers who take care of their issues and come prepared to care for them in a loving open way.

❀ A baby can understand your tone and facial movements, so it's best not to speak of these issues when the baby is in earshot. During the early months of life, a child is discovering that it is okay to just "be." If he senses that it is not okay, his self-esteem may be affected.

Connections and Aspirations

❀ Some women feel guilty for not wanting to be pregnant. If this is happening for you find a safe nonjudgmental person to share your feeling with and make plans to resolve these and other feelings about the pregnancy.

❀ Go ahead and imagine your life path without the baby. You can visit this imaginary path any time you desire. It is normal to want to visit what you thought was going to happen.

❀ Give yourself time to adjust while setting some acceptance goals. For example, you could say to yourself, "In two weeks I will have accepted that (fill in the blank) is not a possibility for my life now." Then work your goal!

❀ Think of the numerous ways you have learned to deal with the unexpected. Consider the skills in adapting you have developed. List all the skills you now have and add them to your résumé. Congratulations!

❀ Keep a list of the things you wish to do in your life and take time to actually write them down. Put the list of dreams and ambitions in a file. Label the file, "Things to do later in life." Do not see having a baby as getting in the way of your dreams! Check that list later.

You may be surprised to find yourself becoming very connected with the baby. Some women feel confused about this strong connection they feel toward their infant. Some report feeling they have abandoned their dreams. If this fits you, you may have found your paradise. Revel in the connection and see where it might lead. Your dreams are not abandoned. Some are on hold; others may be just beginning.

MY JOURNAL:
TURNING OVER A NEW LEAF OF DISCOVERY

I. My Dream Baby and My Real Baby

"Tender are a mother's dreams,
But her babe's not what he seems.
See him plotting in his mind,
To grow up some other kind."
—CLARENCE DAY, *THOUGHTS WITHOUT WORDS*

Write your responses to any or all of the following:

❀ What does your ideal baby look like?

❀ What effect if any is the the dream baby having on your relationship with your real child?

❀ What did you imagine during your childhood about the thought of having a baby?

❀ Did you think you would ever be a mother? Did you imagine that you would be a mother and now can't believe there really is a baby?

❀ What helped you come to terms with the fact that a real live baby was going to be born to you?

❀ Write down the words of assurance you may have said to yourself about accepting your real live baby.

❀ If you "denied" the feeling of overwhelming responsibility, write down how denial helped you.

❁ Are you still denying? If not, what helped you change your coping mechanism?

II. Gifts to Myself

❁ What gifts did you receive during pregnancy that were meant only for you?

❁ What gifts did you receive that were specifically for the baby?

❁ What giving acts did people offer you during pregnancy?

❁ Consider how these gifts helped you give the baby love—unconditional love—that has no price tag. Write down what happened for you that helped you offer unconditional love.

❁ Examine your belief about physical beauty and write how your pregnancy contributed to any changes you may have made in your beliefs.

❁ List the ways you managed the statements from strangers who commented on your pregnant body.

❁ Write down the ways you may have redefined your sexuality based on physical changes, as well as the uses of your sexual organs, during pregnancy.

❁ List the feelings you had about the loss of modesty you went through during pregnancy.

❁ List the ways you coped with the normal physical "ills" of pregnancy. How did you adapt in your emotions to see them as a positive by-product of the pregnancy?

❅ Write down how you instilled confidence in your body's ability to produce a baby.

❅ How did you adapt to the reduction in physical accomplishment you may have experienced in pregnancy? List the ways you coped.

III. Nurture and Self-Esteem

❅ As a journal exercise, look at the following quotation. Consider any feelings you might have and write them down.

"We store nurture droplet by droplet and it is the basis for our self-esteem. Nurture provides humans with attention and contact they need in order to stay alive and live fully."
—JEAN ILLSLEY CLARKE AND CONNIE DAWSON,
GROWING UP AGAIN, PARENTING OURSELVES, PARENTING OUR CHILDREN [4]

CHAPTER 5

Coloring in Your Birth Memories

*"All events except childbirth can be reduced
to a heap of trivia in the end."*
—ANNE TYLER

One of the purposes of this book is to help you ensure as many positive experiences in the child-bearing year as you can. Another is to provide you with tools that can help you resolve negative experiences and see them in a more positive light. By focusing on the bright possibilities of your birthing experience, delivery, postpartum and all that follows, you help yourself and maintain a positive connection with your baby.

Sarah

Sarah had experienced first-trimester spotting with her first baby. Though she went on to deliver a normal, healthy infant, she feared all through her second pregnancy that she might lose the baby because she again experienced early spotting. When her third pregnancy came, it happened again. While she wanted to trust the abilities of her body, she still worried. This nagging concern in the back of her mind was not helped by family members who told her "If it is meant to be, it will be."

To cope with worry and to instill faith, she practiced isolating the components of the pregnancy. She determined the parts of her body that were cooperating and visualized the parts that were not cooperating as strong and healthy. She also wrote a number of reminder Post-it™ notes to focus on seeing her cervix, the part that was causing the spotting, as strong and capable.

Developmental Steps of Labor and Delivery

In her study, "Just Another Day in a Woman's Life?", author Penny Simkin discusses several key emotional steps that can have a dramatic effect on a new mother's emotional development:[1]

❀ Snapshot-like memories
❀ The "halo" effect
❀ Power of the spoken word
❀ Focus on performance
❀ Increased self-esteem

Let's take a look at these components, and as we do, you can relate them to your personal experience.

Snapshot Memories

While the experiences a woman goes through during this time of her life create memories that last all her life, to most women birth is a collection of snapshot-like experiences. These recollections constitute vivid and specific parts of the birthing event. Your mental photo album may be full of emotional recollections of your labor and delivery experience—some inspiring, warmhearted and kind; others, disappointing and painful.

Most new mothers can recall the events of their baby's birth with almost complete accuracy, and their memory of personal response is clear. Emotional responses seem to fall into four distinct groups:

❀ **Positive Pre-Birth Life/Positive Birth**
Most women who had considered their overall life experiences as positive consider birth positive. They tend to thrive in motherhood. A bright birth complements an already bright quality of life.

❀ **Negative Pre-Birth Life/Positive Birth**
Women who had considered their life experiences negative until birth, but who experience birth as positive, tend to thrive in motherhood. It's possible that a happy birth experience may act as an intervention, possibility improving the quality of their lives in their role as mothers.

❀ **Positive Pre-Birth Life/Negative Birth**
Women who had considered their life experiences positive until the time of birth, which they experienced as negative, tended to face challenges in motherhood. A negative birth can negatively affect the quality of a woman's life in her role as a mother.

❀ **Negative Pre-Birth Life/Negative Birth**
Women who had negative life experiences, who also considered the birth of their child as negative, tend to get caught in a treadmill of negative thinking that leads to depression.

Professional research is generally based on a theory, and theories are ideas humans develop to make sense of the world. These conclusions on how pre-birth life coupled with the events of labor and birth make sense to many mothers—those in the Yakima Discovery Group found them fairly accurate. Remember if your perception of your child's birth changes at any time, you can gather support and reframe the experience through the use of material found in this book.

If you don't fit into any of the four groups, you most likely have integrated your memories in a different way. Good for you! You have created your own path to fit your individual needs.

Think a moment about memories of your baby's birth.
Ask yourself these questions:

❀ Are your memories supportive, or not helpful?
❀ Who are the key people in your memories?
❀ What roles do these people play in your emotional health?
❀ Are any of your memories similar to experiences from your past?
❀ In those memories, was there any abuse? Neglect?
❀ Consider how much weight you give to negative memories.
❀ Consider how much weight you give to positive ones.
❀ Are your key memories the ones you want to carry for the rest of your life?

The "Halo" Effect

The halo effect is a protective action performed by the brain of a woman who has just given birth. This miraculous effect keeps you from being overwhelmed by more than you can handle. Just as snapshot memories are like recollections you put together for the whole picture, the halo effect helps you perceive the birth in a radiant, positive light immediately after, and for sometime during, postpartum.

Negative elements of the birth may be temporarily overshadowed by the excitement and joy of the moment. Not until much later does the halo fade, leaving you possibly with less positive memories and emotions associated with the birth. This miracle works very well. The new baby needs to be welcomed and celebrated, and the exhausted new mother needs to focus on the beauty of her precious new child. For awhile, nothing else may seem to matter.

Did the excitement of your baby's birth carry you through your initial postpartum experience? Are you experiencing a halo effect? As with all events in life, the halo effect may wear off. It's hard to say what may trigger the end of this luminiscent period.

The maintenance and renewal of your self-esteem is your job. You can change the path of your self-esteem anytime in your life.

The Power of the Spoken Word

Words spoken to a laboring woman, whether supportive or not, are imprinted in her memory and have long-lasting effects on her overall mental and psychological well-being. Here are comments made to two different women during their labor:

*"You are doing a beautiful job, the baby is almost here.
Keep pushing. I will tell you when to push and when to wait.
You are doing great!"*
—DR. ROGER ROWLES AT THE BIRTH OF KIRSTEN KANYER

". . . He said if I didn't relax, he'd make the stitches too tight and then nothing could get through. You know, he was kind of teasing me, meaning there's no way for any sexual intercourse."
—A PARTICIPANT IN PENNY SIMKIN'S RESEARCH

Because words affect our self-esteem and are strong elements of our snapshot-like memories, it is important to rework negative words and hold on dearly to the positive ones.

Focus on Your Performance

Women who rate their birth experiences as positive tend to view their child's birth as a personal accomplishment or an achievement to be celebrated. When you are in labor, you may hear many inner voices telling you how to accept this miracle.

At this time, your emotional self is torn between excitement and pain. Further, that emotional self has three basic parts, any of which may be operating at any given time. Those three basic parts are: the Parent, the Adult and the Child. Each of these emotional beings inside you has the potential to be helpful or unhelpful.

The Parent acts as an authority figure. She holds all the beliefs that guide you in the world and measures each performance by those beliefs.

The Adult is a human calculator. She makes decisions for today and helps you structure your life and figure things out.

The Child holds all your feelings.

"Each figure has a nurturing side and a critical side. The Critical Parent, for example, will blame, control, protect, punish and boss you. The Nurturing Parent helps, loves, cares, feeds, gives, approves, supports and encourages you."[2]

During labor, because the Parent represents your guiding beliefs, the Critical Parent may have developed a plan for how the labor "should" go. The Critical Parent can emotionally burden you with unhelpful measures of performance that affect your self-esteem and cloud the realities of the birth.

You can reconsider the judgments of this Critical Parent by thinking of your efforts during labor as ways you offered care to your infant. Consider a specific action you performed during labor, like walking around to maximize the effects of the contractions. It's important to look realistically at what you did and document the ways you offered helpful care by doing so. Doing this may help you quiet that Critical Parent and provide you with better options for viewing your performance.

A Birth Plan

Currently, childbirth educators are advocating the use of a birth plan as a communication tool for sharing a woman's wishes for her labor. The tool, originally designed by Penny Simkin, is widely used.

The birth plan is a powerful tool that has offered many women much needed lines of communication with their caregivers. It is a starting place to improve the lines of communication between individuals involved in providing care during labor and birth. It is an overall design, during the childbearing year, for your pregnancy, labor and birth, in which you plan what you want and need and how these steps will proceed.

A birth plan is not a rigid itinerary. As with any plan, it's always advisable to leave room for adjustments. For example, during postpartum, because of the potentially powerful existence of the emotional Critical Parent, it is advisable not to use your birth plan, designed during pregnancy, to evaluate your performance in labor! If you find yourself using it as critical ammunition against yourself, it's best to rid yourself of the plan emotionally and physically.

Increase in Self-Esteem

A positive birth experience can increase a woman's self-esteem and ability to be more assertive in the future.

"I was a person, and then I got married and I became a mother. I had no self-image. When I look back, I see that the only positive experience I had was having those two kids. Those are the things that gave me a sense of myself, and I was able to cope."
—*Simkin Study participant*

Because interpretation of the birth experience may consist of perceptions by her Critical Parent, a woman may miss the opportunity to enhance her self-esteem generated by the positive aspects of the birth experience. The amazing aspects of the birth may be lost and the beauty that lies within the birth event may be overlooked. That's why it's important to your well-being to honestly document the positive elements of the birth and reconsider the negative ones.

 By reevaluating your perceptions, you can sharpen your positive skills and hone your ability to cope.

Self-efficacy centers on a person's judgment of "how well" he or she can execute the course of actions required to deal with a prospective situation. As you know, judgment can be affected by many things and is subjective.

The judgment we make of childbirth is the comparison between what we planned would happen and what actually happened. In postpartum you can resolve these differences with the loving abilities of your Nurturing Parent.

MY JOURNAL:
TURNING OVER A NEW LEAF OF DISCOVERY

Choosing Empowerment—
Reviewing Negative Perceptions

WHEN SELF-ESTEEM SEEMS TO DISAPPEAR, you may choose to behave ineffectively, even though you may know what to do. In the case of childbirth, this means that your perception of the birth may affect the course of your life. A negative perception may affect your ability to make knowledgeable decisions, even when, in your heart and in your mind, you know exactly what course to take.

By personally managing and working through information derived from your experience, you can more readily understand the events of your life and generate new knowledge about them.

Ask yourself and write your thoughts:

❀ What events have occurred that triggered a negative response on my part?

❀ Did I respond negatively because someone said something or did something that brought up old feelings?

❀ If that same event happened today, would I respond the same way?

❀ What would my Nurturing Parent say to me about those feelings?

MY TOOLSHED:
EQUIPMENT TO ENHANCE MY GROWTH & DEVELOPMENT

I. The Time Ball

"Awareness of the past is essential to the maintenance of the purpose in life. Without it we would lack a sense of continuity, and all appreciation of causality, all knowledge of our identity."
—LOWENTHAL

BORN IN THE CULTURE of the Yakama Indian Nation, in Yakima, Washington, the Time Ball was originally used by Yakama women to document their life events on a string woven from hemp. The Time Ball was a marker for all of the precious, monumental episodes in their lives.

Beginning at her marriage, and continuing throughout her life, a Yakama woman would add to her Time Ball any event that held significance to her and her family. Documenting her trials and accomplishments, the Time Ball was a wonderful kinesthetic tool that documented a connection between all the historical events of her life. As the first written form of history, the Time Ball functioned like a diary for vital lessons of tribal events.[3]

For the Yakamas, connection between people and events was and is an essential way to develop an appreciation for and an understanding of life.

The self-efficacy of a new mother can be affected by the events of her childbearing experience, which can cause her to feel unsure of herself and occasionally be unwilling to advocate for herself and her child.

II. Your Personal Time Ball

Here are the steps to creating your own Time Ball. It's an exercise designed for you to do alone, but you are welcome to do it in the company of others.

❀ **Step 1:** Choose some string. It can be a leather tong, beautifully colored yarn, ribbons, a piece of cloth from clothing now too tattered to wear, or some embroidery floss that you braid to make a strong string. Make sure that it's thin enough to string beads onto.

❀ **Step 2:** Gather some pretty beads, feathers, rocks with holes, to mark the significant events of your life.

❀ **Step 3:** Decide on a starting point, a significant event to begin your Time Ball. You might choose your own birth, when you turned 16 or 21 years old, when you got married or when you met the your life mate. Choose any event you wish to be your starting point.

❀ **Step 4:** Tie a knot in the string to mark your significant starting event. Then consider as many significant events as you can recall that have followed.

❀ **Step 5:** For each event, tie a knot or series of knots; then string on a bead separated by knots, feathers, hair, twigs or threads from significant articles of clothing. These are only suggesions. The possibilities are endless.

❀ **Step 6:** Begin to roll the string up like a ball. You can unravel the ball at any time to retrace your life events.

❀ **Step 7:** Enjoy learning to appreciate, understand and read meaning into the knots, beads and other memorabilia in your Time Ball. Spend time reading and rereading your ball to enhance your memory of each event.

❀ **Step 8:** As you experience new events, add them. Each time you add to the Time Ball, spend time reading the previous knots and unraveling your life story.

❀ **Step 9:** When you run out of string, weave in more.

❀ **Step 10:** Once you have documented several events, get together with a trusted support person to tell your story. This documents your self-efficacy—the belief in your personal power.

When maneuvering through such dramatic events, both negative and positive, the Time Ball may help you marvel at what an amazing survivor you are. The Time Ball may help you make sense of your experiences and acknowledge that you did the best you possibly could do at the time.

The Time Ball helps you trace the events of your childbearing journey. Your story can be told and retold, offering continual understanding of how you are affected by your legacy and providing a deep appreciation for the person you are.

> **The story told in the threads of the Time Ball**
> **give evidence to your earlier values about the birth**
> **and your commitment to how the birth played out.**

As the Time Ball grows and is rolled up, many of the recorded events are hidden from view. Similar to the stages of human development, you cannot see all the events knotted on your Time Ball, but you know they are there. Although hidden from view, they exist in time and space and affect who you are. Through growth, change, celebration and pain, you capture your unique efforts and abilities in life. Your efforts were real, not just chance or good luck. You really did an amazing job in birthing your baby!

MY TOOLSHED:
EQUIPMENT TO ENHANCE MY GROWTH & DEVELOPMENT

III. Childbirth Flashbacks

HERE ARE SOME OTHER TOOLS to help you work through your childbirth memories. Focus on the questions that hold most meaning for you. Invite a friend over to discuss them, or use them in a Discovery Group.

❀ Are you now "flashing back" to the birth of your child and finding circumstances not as helpful as you initially remembered?

❀ If you are flashing back to the birth of your child, what memories or experiences seem to not be helpful now? List them.

❀ What are some alternative ways caregivers could have offered you care that would have made you feel more supported?

❀ Are there events that occurred that are negative but were completely out of anyone's control?

❀ Are you blaming yourself for not preventing them?

Some Notes to Remember:

❀ During the birth of your baby, you deserve helpful support and nurture.

❀ You survived one of the most dramatic events known to humankind and did the best job you could.

❀ You are an amazing survivor who found ways to strive and thrive in a major life crisis.

MY JOURNAL:
TURNING OVER A NEW LEAF OF DISCOVERY

 Words to Soothe You

LOOK AT THE FOLLOWING QUESTIONS. Mark the ones you would like to think about or discuss. Write in your journal, or in this book, your responses to the following:

❀ Were there words spoken to you that you found supportive? What were they?

❀ Were words spoken to you that were not supportive? If yes, what were they and how did you interpret them?

❀ List the words you hold dear to your heart, that inspired you and instilled a feeling of confidence.

❀ Write the words you wish you had heard.

❀ What would you like to change about your birth experience in terms of the way you see your performance?

❀ What do you think you did well during labor?

❀ Are you finding that you created a realistic birth plan?

❀ Are you using your birth plan as a measuring stick of your performance?

❀ Write yourself some true affirmations to balance the critical words that you may be hearing related to your performance.

❀ What do you see as your greatest accomplishment during the birth of the baby?

❀ What did you do that made the birth the positive event it was?

❀ What events affect your feeling of negative self-esteem or positive self-esteem related to the birth?

❀ Have you been aware of a sense of increased personal power, or has your sense of personal power decreased since the birth?

CHAPTER 6

Harvesting Your Postpartum Horizon

"Weeping may remain for a night,
but rejoicing comes in the morning."
—PSALMS 30:5

The goal of your postpartum journey is twofold:[1]

❀ To develop a profound sense of responsibility for your child.
❀ To reclaim your adult self as a mother.

Denying your feelings—whether positive or negative—can make adjustment to parenting take longer. By reviewing this emotional destination on your postpartum journey, you'll become acutely aware of your successes and challenges along the way.

Following is a shopping list of things to look for as you move through your postpartum garden. It's outlined by the age of your child, so you may want to read only through the age you are now experiencing. That way, you can grow at your own pace. Naturally, you may read beyond if you wish.

Consider your personality temperament as you go. It may be helpful for those of you who are introverts to talk over your findings with a member of your support team. Extraverts may wish to find a support group to discuss the information. You may also choose to draw or write your responses in your journal, or use the Pop-Bead Tool to understand associations. There are many ways to seek solutions to life's challenges.

1 The First Month: Inward Focus

While in this initial section of your postpartum garden, it's normal for you to focus inward on yourself and be aware of the attention given to you rather than to your baby.

If there are steps you have already completed, move ahead to another. If there are steps you feel are not helpful, you can write in your journal your responses to them.

Typically a New Mother May Accomplish Some of the Following Steps:

❀ Recount your birth story. (See "My Toolshed: Equipment to Enhance My Growth and Development" on page 123.)

❀ Request abundant amounts of nurture and care from your support team.

❀ Begin to accept your baby's personality, looks and sex. Tuck the dream baby away.

❀ Adjust to your post-pregnancy body and new physical sensations—tightening of the womb, filling of your breast with milk or discomfort from your healing body.

❀ Monitor postpartum emotional changes, which may be the result of a drop in hormone level combined with the dramatic physical challenges listed above.

❀ Grieve the loss of your pregnancy.

❀ Believe there really is a baby.

❀ Learn how to take the best care of your baby.

❀ Look for support for becoming a mother.

❀ Resolve the balancing act of taking care of your household by getting help or accepting help from your support team. New mothers deserve a babymoon, a restful time to recuperate from the birth and adjust to new motherhood.

> *"If she moves through this time without fulfilling these needs*
> *for self-absorption and without sharing her emotions,*
> *they may linger on and be incorrectly interpreted*
> *by the woman's own self-indulgent inadequacy as a mother."*
> —SALLY PLACKSIN, MOTHERING THE NEW MOTHER

2 The Second Month: Captivated by Your Baby

By the second month, most women begin to see a pattern develop and feel a sense of love toward their babies. The tiny stranger is becoming more familiar.

Typically a New Mother May Accomplish
Some of the Following Steps:

❀ Move from concern for yourself to becoming captivated with
your baby. The baby's increased ability to fixate on its mother
brings the relationship to a deeper level.

❀ Begin to experience a strong, emotional connectedness with your
baby. This process is assisted by fond memories of being loved by
your own mother. If you do not have such memories, you can
choose to love the baby and build new memories together.

❀ Begin to match your feelings with the reality of motherhood:
"I am a mother!" "Can you say 'Mama'?"

❀ Withdraw from the happenings of the outside world to gain
protection from the "ills" of the world for yourself and your baby.

❀ Begin to actively problem-solve concerns relating to your baby's
behavior, especially sleeping and feeding issues.
"Will I ever sleep again?"
"This baby nurses so much. I wonder if I have enough milk?"

"O young thing, your mother's lovely armful!
How sweet the fragrance of your body!"
—EURIPIDES

3 & 4 The Third and Fourth Months: Symbiosis

Psychologist Margaret Mahler defines symbiosis as "dual unity,"
where both—the baby and the mother—are seen as extensions of
each other. The baby sees its mother as an extension of itself, one

who fulfills needs and gratifies wishes. The mother perceives the baby as still very much part of herself.

Typically a New Mother May Accomplish Some of the Following Steps:

❀ Notice how you describe the baby as part of yourself:
"When we nurse . . ."
"We're starting to sit up.
"I think we might be getting a tooth."
"We're really starting to know who Daddy is."

❀ Notice how you gain accuracy in building skills for interpreting your baby's cries. You may find yourself responding successfully to the baby's desires more often. You may feel a great deal of pride in this and insist on others using the same methods you have found helpful.

❀ Recognize how you miss your baby during times of separation. "Honey, I can't wait to get back to the baby. Can we go home now?"

❀ Find yourself deeply gazing lovingly eye-to-eye with your baby.

❀ Take notice of how you find the baby more interesting than anything else, whether or not you have returned to work or are staying home.

❀ Make continuing contributions to your baby's emotional sense of well-being through smiling, touching and talking to him or her.

❀ Do you feel a fear of isolation? Begin to actively seek out other mothers as a reflection of yourself and to supply your need for adult companionship.

❊ Analyze the effects of loss of control in your life. The baby may have an erratic schedule, you may have placed expectations and demands on yourself and find that things are not going as you expected.

5 The Fifth Month: Expanding Your World

During the fifth month, the baby begins to realize there is more to life than mom. This baby who was once willing to nurse without distraction will interrupt feedings at the slightest noise. The five-month-old who two months ago would rather snuggle and cuddle now wants to stand on mother's lap looking at what there is to see.

The baby's growth and development propel the mother into a new developmental phase that moves her attention back to herself. During this time, the baby becomes more curious about the world; and the mother, curious about who she is. As the new mother now observes that the infant is not as dependent on her to meet all his interests, she begins to wonder who *she* is. As in adolescence, she may experience an "identity crisis." If this sounds familiar:

Typically a New Mother May Accomplish Some of the Following Steps:

❊ Acknowledge the first of many steps toward independence that your baby is taking as she or he begins to explore the environment.

❊ Celebrate that your baby is becoming her/his own person, even while you mourn the passage of the precious earliest moments of infancy you experienced together.

❀ Your baby's newfound independence and interest in the surroundings may be causing you to contemplate what the reduced need for you might mean to your life and to your identity.

❀ Acknowledge feelings of agitation, restlessness and discontent as you begin to focus on new thoughts that define who you are.

❀ If returning to work, you may be evaluating how to try to balance motherhood with work. You may also begin to see how the two define your identity.

❀ If you are staying home to care for your infant, you may be wondering if that's all there is to life. While you may see your life as running smoothly, the components of your daily routine may not be adding up to what you consider as "valuable" on a worldly scale.

❀ Consider your adult relationship with the father of the baby. This may mean considering your sexuality, based on the desire to resume the relationship that was present before the birth of the baby.

❀ Are you experiencing conflict in your relationship related to sexuality? You may be attempting to figure out how a mother behaves sexually. Becoming a mother changes your sexuality, as it does your identity. Because human sexuality is related to identity, during this time when you are redefining your identity, sexuality may be an issue of conflict.

❀ You may be feeling a desire to be left alone to figure things out. You may also be looking for some way to escape the demands of the baby, the household, work and your love relationship in order to begin the task of defining who you are as a person. You may need to juggle your pre-motherhood expectations as you resolve the dilemma of how to make everything fit.

❀ This is a time to look at the way all elements of family life are connected to you—the baby, your husband, your work, hobbies, outside relationships, religious activities. Your feelings surrounding these elements may lead to a deep sense of loss. Remember feelings of sadness can accompany any time of dramatic change, this is a normal response to all the changes.

> *"I used to lie long hours with the baby in my arms, watching her asleep; sometimes catching a gaze from her eyes; feeling very near the edge, the mystery, perhaps the knowledge of life . . ."*
> —ISADORA DUNCAN

6 & 7 The Sixth and Seventh Months: I Can Be Me and a Mother Too

By the beginning of the sixth month and continuing through the seventh, a new mother feels that some part of her life has ended, while another part has begun. She most likely has begun to sew up her identity issues and come to understand the events of the past six months better in relation to who she is.

The care of her baby and her family is a job she begins to accept as part of who she is. During these months, a new mother may begin to feel more comfortable with the idea that she is now a mother.

Typically a New Mother May Accomplish Some of the Following Steps:

❀ Rather than wanting time all to yourself to ponder your identity, you may now be focusing on fun things to do or self-nurturing activities, such as taking a long bath or reading a book—on something other than babies.

❀ You may be finding that your skills in caring for your child seem to be automatic and more natural.

❀ Many babies at this age begin to feed on a more regular schedule, assisted by the introduction of solid food. The bottle or breastfeeding sessions may have decreased during the day. Nighttime feeding may increase because the baby is busy during the day. You may have a number of reactions to the waking older baby—from pleasure about being able to spend quiet moments together, to anger over interrupted sleep.

❀ You may be feeling more confident that others can provide care and interpret your baby's signals, which has created an interest in having time away from the infant.

❀ While you may have wondered who you are, in the sixth and seventh months, you may begin to feel a direction to your life and seek time away to integrate your sense of self.

❀ You may consider returning to work or seeking social activities outside of the home that you can call your own.

❀ Exercising and regaining your pre-pregnancy body may be a big priority as you resolve the changes in your body that took place as a result of the childbearing year.

❀ You may acquire more interest in talking about yourself and your life rather than focusing your conversations exclusively on the baby.

❀ You may find the baby's abilities to entertain herself as a welcome break rather than a threat to your identity as a mother.

❀ The baby's father's participation in the life of the family may be of great interest to you as you begin to understand that family life is definitely part of your identity.

❀ You may be looking more realistically at the emotionally and physically exhausting aspects of caring for an infant.

❀ The need for additional information on how to care for the growing baby, manage the elements of family life and balance your emerging identity will move you to seek other women like you who are parenting similar-aged children.

❀ Seeing the baby grow, you may feel overwhelmed by the responsibility for the child's development and how the quality of family life may affect his or her development.

❀ Financial issues may be on your mind as you experience strong feelings related to the realities of the cost of family life.

"In spite of the cost of living,
having a child is still popular."
—AUTHOR UNKNOWN

8 & 9 The Eighth and Ninth Months: Together Again

As the baby grows and becomes more active, a mother is forced to see her different role, now almost one of a consultant, advising the tiny explorer who maneuvers through the world. This relationship is very different from the relationship four months before. Mother and child now see themselves as two separate individuals.

Typically a New Mother May Accomplish Some of the Following Steps:

❀ Seeing yourself as separate from your baby, you becomes a touchstone for reassurance to your new explorer.

❀ You feel comfortable with this new role as the baby practices new skills and you offer supportive care through encouragement and assertive care by ensuring a safe environment to explore.

❀ This is a time for evaluating the breastfeeding relationship and finding a way to decide whether to quit or continue.

❀ Because the baby is more active, you may experience difficulty with nursing or even bottle-feeding.

❀ Feelings of rejection may creep in as the baby attempts to wean. Because the feeding sessions are so different from the newborn feeding schedule, you may feel confused. The baby may not request the breast as often, sadly, many babies are weaned at nine months for this reason. It is not necessary to make this decision now. You might wait to see if things change.

❀ Feelings of relief may be prevalent as the baby goes through new developmental stages.

❀ You may find this time fun as you begin to teach the baby about the world.

❀ Feelings of knowledge and awareness are aroused as you recount with a fair amount of objectivity the picture of who your little one is. This assessment often includes a complete description of activities, routine and personality style.

❀ You may find yourself resolving feelings and looking for options related to the separation and stranger anxiety your baby may be going through.

❀ Look for feelings of excitement as you continue to integrate your role as a mother into your understanding of who you are.

❀ Notice any feelings of community with other women who have become mothers—a sisterhood of sorts.

❀ Most mothers will begin to celebrate and understand the line of generations that result from parenting. Appreciating your new place in your extended family group is part of the motherhood process.

You have just completed the journey of becoming a mother. With the skills you have acquired to plant your new family-garden you can move to other challenges that family life may bring.

**As you continue on your journey in gardening,
practice seeing yourself as the lovable
and capable person you are.**

MY TOOLSHED:
EQUIPMENT TO ENHANCE MY GROWTH & DEVELOPMENT

The Structure Highway

A Tool to Evaluate the Safety and Protection You Received

DURING THE CHILDBEARING YEAR, you need clear and specific guidelines for your self care. Information on weight gain, the use of chemicals, recommendations about rest and exercise are all topics that fit into the "Structure Highway." They are also examples of areas that a person needs to consider when establishing healthy boundaries. Structure during the childbearing year is a way in which your support team set boundaries related to health care and safety issues so that you can establish a sense that you are protected and cared for.

During the childbearing year, there are many ways in which your support team can offer boundaries in order to provide you with protection and care. They might change the cat box to help you avoid the possibility of harmful infections passing to your baby, or check that the paint used to refurbish baby furniture does not contain toxic chemicals. These are two examples of offering healthy structure.

Clear, positive rules and boundaries related to your health and well-being help to build a framework for you to nurture your baby and enhance your self-esteem. Nonnegotiable and negotiable structure rules related to your health care offer you a chance to feel safe and cared for . . . and to feel loved!

Jean Illsley Clark and Connie Dawson, authors of *Growing Up Again, Parenting Ourselves, Parenting Our Children,* describe structure in this way:

Both physically and emotionally, we need the safety and protection of "structure" to survive. The opposite of structure is chaos. Structure helps us to function effectively. Structure (offers us direction) to do tasks skillfully; to think clearly; to collect and assess information; to identify options; to set goals; to organize; to start, and to complete tasks, to manage materials, tools, time, ideas and feelings; to be responsible, to honor commitments and to develop morals and values.

Structure creates a strong boundary that insures people will keep themselves safe from harm and for getting their needs met.[2]

The authors also include this extended definition:

Structure also helps people to become aware of their limits . . . it involves teaching of rules and offers helpful information. It also outlines consequences for boundaries or rules that are disregarded or broken.[3]

Learning about helpful structure during your childbearing year will renew rules you may have learned as a child—rules that can benefit you now as a parent. Or it may be that learning now about structure may be the first exposure you have had to it. The structure offered by physicians, nurses, childbirth educators and parenting instructors can help you live a more secure life related to your personal well-being and health. Later, when you recall positive structure you received during your childbearing year, your memories of these positive experiences can help enhance your feelings of self-esteem.

In its original form, Clarke and Dawson organized "The Structure Highway" from left to right, in order of "strictness." I have maintained this order to help you discover and label the limits and rules you experienced related to your health, safety and well-being.

The authors explain:

> "Rigidity" is the most strict, while "abandonment" offers no care at all. While rigidity and abandonment are at opposite ends of the chart, the effects are similar. Each style ignores the needs you may have for care and support.

> In contrast, Nonnegotiable Rules and Negotiable Rules are the positive structure patterns that support working cooperatively to offer boundaries to support your wellness and the wellness of your baby.

When examining the Structure Highway on pages 120 and 121 be aware of the following points:

❀ Each lane of the highway represents the responses you could have received from your support team.

❀ Each one of us will respond to each lane differently, hearing or seeing the responses from our unique perspective. Because of this, your responses may not exactly match those on the chart.

❀ You may have received combinations of all lanes on the highway from many different sources during the childbearing period as well as throughout your life.

❀ Structure is a skill that parents need to expand. By receiving positive structure from your caregivers and support persons during the childbearing year, you gain knowledge of skills such as self-care, family management, vocational work skills and child-rearing techniques. For the new mother, the structure she received during her childbearing journey provides her with a guideline to live a healthy life that leads to feelings that she is loved, important and capable.

Steps to Using the Structure Highway

❀ **Step 1**—Write down a situation related to your health and safety. For example, the situation could be about recommended rules you received that were part of your medical care plan:

Let us say your physician was telling you about the possibility of your having an episiotomy. He or she may have insisted without exception on the use of an episiotomy to deliver the baby. "All my patients get an episiotomy. It's the way I practice medicine; it is not an option in your care."

❀ **Step 2**—Read through each of the columns offered on the Structure Highway (pages 120 and 121) and determine which one describes a situation similar to the physican's attitude about episiotomies.

The physician's statement in the example, may have sounded like "rigidity." The comment as stated was set in stone, indicating that the topic was nonnegotiable and that the doctor was not open to hearing your ideas and feelings.

❀ **Step 3**—Think about how you wish the physician's explanation had been given.

Your physician could have used "nonnegotiable rules" such as, "It has been my experience with women who have a pelvis size similar to yours and have a baby the size that you are carrying, that it is safer to perform an episiotomy. I plan to do an episiotomy to ensure your health and the health of your baby."

Or, your doctor could have used "negotiable rules" such as, "I consider the use of an episiotomy on a case-by-case basis. There have been cases when it has been helpful and times when it has been unnecessary. When we get to the point in your labor where I might consider it, I will discuss it with you and look for options based on the events the labor is presenting us."

Consider what effect the kind of structure you received may have had on your emotional well-being, or think of other alternatives to the response you were offered.

❀ **Step 4**—Based on the definitions in the columns on the Structure Highway, rewrite the responses you received in a way that would have been more supportive to you. Have someone read your responses back to you and listen for the differences.

❀ **Step 5**—Evaluate the effects on your emotional self of the care you received. Do you get positive feelings about the care you received? How much value, negative or positive, do these memories have for you. Are they strong, negative, snapshot-like memories, or warm, positive, energizing ones? Considering your feelings about the structure you received, can you see some effect on your self-esteem as a mother?

If you determine that there is a negative effect, make plans to resolve the issue. You may choose to seek support from a therapist, a clergy member, a support group or a member of your support team. You may simply need your feelings validated and to look for other more supportive alternatives. And remember to congratulate yourself for reworking the issue!

THE STRUCTURE HIGHWAY

RIGIDITY

Characteristics:

It is typically made up of old rules or medical procedures that are "written in concrete." It may consist of outdated procedures that the caregiver still insists on without exception. These old rules and procedures ignore your needs to develop, your needs to maintain dignity, and may sound too strict to you. Because they may not fit logically for today, they may ignore your ability to think and feel sure about what you know. Rigid boundaries can seem to be offered for your "welfare," but come from fear inside of the people offering it because they may not be comfortable with new methods. Sometimes this type of structure is accompanied by a withdrawal of love or care, as a consequence for not following the rule for allowing the procedure. Rigid care may be accompanied with threats of abuse. The person offering this type of structure does not believe that you should have any say in working on the situation.

People Who Experience Rigidity May Hear the Following Underlying Messages:

You are not important. Don't think. Don't be. You will be abandoned if you do not allow the procedure or if you do not follow the "rule." Don't trust your own abilities.

Common Responses of People Who Experience Rigidity:

You may feel oppressed, distanced, angry, scared, hopeless, imperfect, discounted, mistrusted, abandoned, no-good.

Decision About Self-Esteem Often Made by People Who Experience Rigidity:

I am not wanted. This person does not care for me and my desires. The rules or procedure are more important than my needs. Others are supposed to think for me. I may feel a need to comply or rebel or withdraw. I blame myself for the care I am given.

CRITICISM

Characteristics:

Criticism uses labels consisting of bad names rather than showing helpful ways for maintaining the relationship or to get help. Criticism uses global words such as "never" and "always." It tells you how to fail, by mentioning all that is negative in a situation. Criticism negates those who receive it. Ridicule, which presents a bitter and mocking invitation for hurtful laughter, is a devastating form of critical care. Those who use criticism believe that by outlining all the negative points in a situation the person who receives the criticism will automatically be motivated to look for another alternative. Unfortunately, people hear criticism as something negative about themselves and may not see the other alternatives toward helpful structure.

People Who Experience Criticism May Hear the Following Underlying Message:

Don't be who you are. Don't be successful. Don't be capable. You are not lovable.

Common Responses of People Who Experience Criticism:

Feelings of being powerless, diminished, rejected, hurt, humiliated, squashed, angry, unimportant, inadequate, scared or discounted.

Decisions About Self-Esteem Often Made by People Who Experience Criticism:

I have to know what you don't know, I will have to try harder to be strong, or to be perfect. If I don't do things right I am a bad person. I can't be good enough. I am hopeless, so why bother?

NONNEGOTIABLE RULES

Characteristics:

Reasonable Nonnegotiable rules are boundaries which assist in building your self-esteem because they insure health and well-being. These rules support a childbearing woman's need to have a safe passage for herself and her baby. Because the structure must be followed for your health or safety, it offer supportive protection. This type of structure offered can be changed to benefit your welfare, or changed based on new factual and up-to-date information.

People Who Experience Nonnegotiable Care or Support May Hear the Following Underlying Message:

You welfare and safety are important. Your support team is willing and able to be responsible to enforce this helpful, non-negotiable set of rules to insure your health and the health of your infant. Your support team will be responsible for informing you of the medical procedures that are necessary and not negotiable. Your support team will also support your decisions about care and welcome your questions and requests for additional information supporting your curiosity and need for information.

Common Responses of People Who Experience Nonnegotiable Rules:

Feelings of safety, being cared for, helped, supported and accounted for. You may feel frustrated and resistant at times when you question the nonnegotiable rules in order to determine if the rule is really necessary.

Decisions About Self-Esteem Often Made by People Who Experience Nonnegotiable Care:

There are some ways of being cared for that I must follow. I am a good person. I am lovable and capable. My support team cares about me and they are willing to help take care of me.

Adapted from *Growing Up Again, Parenting Ourselves, Parenting Our Children*, by Jean Illsley Clarke and Connie Dawson, ©1989 by Jean Illsley Clarke and Connie Dawson. Adapted by permission of Hazelden Foundation, Center City, MN.

Negotiable Rules
Characteristics:
Negotiable structure helps you to think clearly and to problem solve. This type of care or support is negotiated between the client/patient and the caregiver and then reinforced based on the circumstances presented. This type of structure supports nonnegotiable care, allows for adjustment to accommodate circumstances. The process of negotiation helps you to argue and hassle with caregivers and support people on points that are important to you. It helps you to clarify your beliefs and positions on your care and the care of your baby. It helps you to decide to learn to be responsible for yourself and your family in new ways. It also provides a supportive structure that helps to avoid the pitfalls of black and white—good or bad—thinking related to the many choices of how to solve problems during the childbearing year. It offers chances to think of many solutions to problems rather than locking in on one. It allows you an opportunity to ask for information from many sources and supports a belief that you can find ways that work well in your family group.

People Who Experience Negotiable Rules May Hear the Following Underlying Messages:
You can think, negotiate and initiate your care and support. Your needs are important and other people's needs are important. You can manage things as they really exist, in the here and now. You are expected to use your personal power in ways that are positive and life enhancing, for yourself and others.

Common Responses of People Who Experience Negotiable Rules:
Feelings of respect, of being cared for, listened to, powerful, important, loved, intelligent, safe and sometimes, frustrated, as you maneuver through the negotiation process. You begin to learn how to evaluate information, how to take part in making a care/support plan as well as how to follow through with the plan. Experiencing "Negotiable Structure" helps you to learn about being responsible and flexible.

Decisions About Self-Esteem Often Made by People Who Experience Negotiable Care:
It is okay to ask for care and to be dependent at times, especially during the childbearing year. I can think things through and get help in making decisions. I can work cooperatively with other adults. As a new mother I can increase my abilities to be responsible for my care and support. I am competent.

Marshmallow
Characteristics:
Marshmallow grants freedom without an expectation of responsible behavior on your part. It may sound supportive, but it implies that you are not capable of negotiating or keeping rules. It discounts your adult abilities and gives you permission to fail, to be irresponsible, to be helpless and hopelessly not providing reasonable health rules. At the same time it makes the caregiver or support person look good because they are "going easy on you." It also allows them to play the martyr by letting others take advantage of them, or to feel in control of the situation by setting up a circumstance where you will fail without helpful rules.

People Who Experience Marshmallow May Hear the Following Underlying Messages:
Don't be competent or responsible. Don't be the thinking capable person you are. Don't grow up. You can have your way by acting childlike and obnoxious. Take care of the caregiver or support person rather than ask for necessary help for yourself. The needs of the caregiver are more important than your needs.

Common Responses of People Who Experience Marshmallow:
Feelings of being patronized or kept little. Encouragement to be incompetent in order to please the caregiver or support person. Feeling of being crazy because of the mixed messages like, "Oh, you can do what you want," or "You are taking advantage of me." Feeling of being undermined, manipulated, discounted, uncared for, unsatisfied and angry.

Decisions About Self-Esteem Often Made by People Who Experience Marshmallow:
I must take care of other peoples' feelings and needs instead of my own. I don't need to care about anyone but myself because no one is encouraging me to ask for what I need. I am not capable of learning how to take care of myself. If someone offers help or care, there is an expectation that I will have to pay for it in some way. I can't expect to receive helpful structure from my caregiver or my support team.

Abandonment
Characteristics:
Abandonment consists of the lack of a clear care plan, no protection and no contact or support. The caregiver or support team are not available for you. Sometimes teasing is offered, which is a form of abandonment.

People Who Experience Abandonment May Hear the Following Underlying Messages:
I am not willing to take care of you. I don't want to help you. Your needs are not important. No one is here for you. You do not exist.

Common Responses of People Who Experience Abandonment:
Feelings of rage, fright, terror, hurt, anger. Other feelings may include feeling rejected, discounted, baffled, unimportant, upset, like not being alive.

Decisions About Self-Esteem Often Made by People Who Experience Abandonment:
Don't expect or ask for help. No one cares. If I am to survive this experience, I will have to do it myself. If offered help, mistrust it. Help and trust are a joke.

MY JOURNAL:
TURNING A NEW LEAF OF DISCOVERY

 Discovery in the Garden—
One Woman's Harvest

HERE IS A TESTIMONY from Andrea Boroff Egan's book *The Newborn Mother*. Consider what Ellen, the author of this story experienced. Write a positive discovery you made recently.

> Nothing that has ever happened to me before has transformed me so completely. I'm different in every way I can think of. I don't look very different, but I have a different sense of my body, and its power. I gave birth with this body, I nourished a baby with it. I was terrified at the beginning, and I overcame my fear. I knew nothing, nothing about being a mother but I learned.
>
> I got through going back to work, and changing jobs. Got through what seemed like the end of my sex life forever, got through a huge upheaval with my marriage, and I feel like we are better friends for what we've been through together.
>
> I walk down the street and see other mothers and feel like I am one of them—like we all know something. I feel like I just emerged, like a butterfly must feel coming out of the cocoon—a metamorphosis. I look at myself in the mirror and I recognize myself, and I feel proud, very proud of myself.[4]

❀ Name a positive discovery you made recently.

MY TOOLSHED:
EQUIPMENT TO ENHANCE MY GROWTH & DEVELOPMENT

Telling Your Story

ANDREA EAGAN in her groundbreaking book documenting the developmental stages of new mothers, *The Newborn Mother*, says that a woman who has recently had a baby needs to talk about it. The experience of birthing a baby is phenomenal, and a mother knows instinctively that she has indisputably become someone new. Most women feel driven to recount the story over and over again.

The telling of one's birth story is part of the natural emotional development and a step that must not be missed. Here are some recommendations:

❀ **Step 1:** Secure many opportunities to talk about the birth. Telling your birth story is as important a development step as learning to crawl is for the baby.

❀ **Step 2:** Write down the events of the birth to help you recall them. Write them in the form of a letter to yourself or to your child.

❀ **Step 3:** Tell your story at different times. Shortly after the birth you'll have many chances, but continue to tell it for months and years to come.

❀ **Step 4:** Consider asking someone to use active listening skills by mirroring back to you some of your thoughts. You may gain deeper insights into the emotional effects of the birth if someone helps by saying some of your ideas back to you for clarification and deeper investigation.

❀ **Step 5:** Design or seek a support group to talk more about the baby's birth. Hearing birth stories is a wonderful way to support one another and to gain perspective on this unforgettable event.

❀ **Step 6:** If you discover, in the telling, some detours, consider using some of the suggestions you're finding in this book to resolve any negative experiences you recall.

 Remember: *Never use language that indicates the baby is the cause of the events of labor. It has been documented that humans can feel guilt from overhearing their parents' conversations about them. In truth, the baby was the result, not the cause, of your labor to go one way or another.*

MY JOURNAL:
TURNING OVER A NEW LEAF OF DISCOVERY

I. The Journey

WRITE IN YOUR JOURNAL as if you were talking to your best friend. This is a treasure to keep forever, and you'll be able to recall your thoughts and feelings whenever you like.

"Preserve the old, but know the new."
—CHINESE PROVERB

❀ Write down your childbearing story. This may help to validate what you have gone through.

❀ Use mind mapping to help you organize your thoughts and feelings and get them on paper. See the "Mind Mapping" exercise below.

❀ Write a poem, a letter, a story or an essay about any aspect of your childbearing journey.

II. Mind Mapping[5]

In this technique, the creative abilities are used to organize a series of problems and feelings connected to that problem in a way that allows constructive mental patterns to come forth. Try it to help solve a problem, discover the root of a problem, or simply to examine your thoughts.

Equipment you'll need:
- Paper
- Felt-tip markers

Instructions:

❀ In the middle of a page, write and circle a word or two to describe the problem, concern or issue the you wish to consider.

❀ Let your mind wander.

❀ Each time you think of a new idea connected to the issue, draw a spoke out from the center and write the idea at the end of the line.

❀ Now circle that new word-thought. (Instead of words you may also draw symbols that describe the new idea.)

❀ Continue using the same process, drawing smaller branches off the main spokes to indicate new, more detailed ideas connecting to each of the spokes. You will begin to see relationships between the elements of the problem.

❀ You may choose to use different colored felt-tip markers to further code the associations and their importance to each element of the issue.

At some point you may see a pattern or a frequent idea emerging from the mind map. This may help you to identify where to begin to work through a problem. Take your time developing the map. Attempt to get the whole picture before drawing any conclusions or formatting solutions. Neatness definitely does NOT count! Finding solutions does!

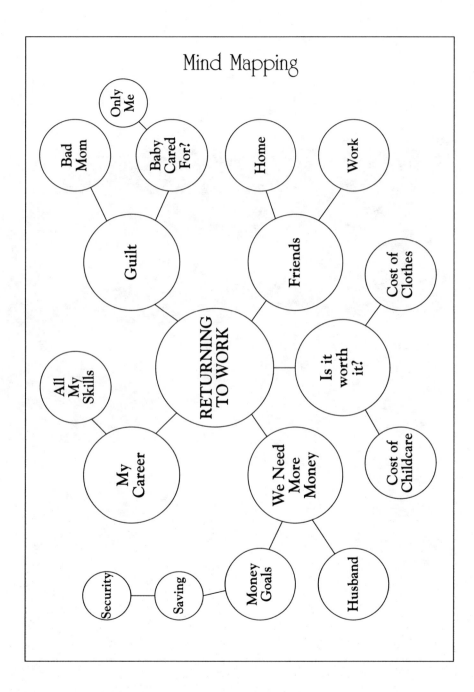

Recycling Communication Paths

*"Everything comes of itself at the appointed time.
This is the meaning of heaven and earth."*
—THE I CHING

Have you ever experienced *déjà-vu*—the feeling that what is happening now has happened before? In the world of psychology, *déjà-vu* is often looked upon as a form of recycling.

Recycling[1] offers us the chance to smooth out the wrinkles in our childhood and other past history using the benefit of more advanced and sophisticated adult skills. At no time does this happen more often than when people become parents. Apparently our own recycling is especially stimulated during the development of our children as they advance through stages of human development.

A Gift from Nature

Watching our kids grow can subconsciously remind us of ourselves as little ones. Sometimes this can be traumatic, which is why new parents often need the supportive care of others. That care includes collecting positive strokes, taking comfort, using affirmations and visualizing success.

Most human beings receive some care during childhood that is helpful and some that is not. When a woman becomes a parent, she has an opportunity to recycle the developmental stages of her own childhood. It is truly a gift from nature that parents can use the growth and development of their children as tools for self-discovery and recovery from the pain of their own past.

"Recycling provides the opportunity to look at early childhood tasks at an older age and perceive them in more grown-up ways. Exciting in its possibilities, the assurance that you have more than one chance in life to get what you need and many chances to resolve your problems can be very reassuring."[2]

Recycling is nature's renewal period. It's a time to weed out past years' mistakes, repair the soil and replant. It's a process that provides a chance to create new patterns for living.

**When you find it difficult to care for your child(ren)
or feel lost on the path of parenthood,
you may be recycling.**

Here is a classic example of recycling. The scars, pain of unmet needs of a woman named Jessica, are provoked later when she has a child.

Jessica & Lacey

Jessica was a bright, intelligent, outgoing, creative child of six. Yet, first grade was a virtual storm for her. She moved, her mother remarried, she experienced the birth of a sibling, and her teacher, who despised her, put her at the farthest desk in the room.

She grew up in spite of all this. Whatever potholes she experienced in her development, she buried well out of her awareness. When the time came 21 years later to send her daughter, Lacey, off to first grade, Jessica was a mess. Even though her daughter was a bright, outgoing child, Jessica was sure there was trouble on the horizon. She was sure the teacher would dislike her little girl, and that other children would tease and mock her daughter.
To Jessica, school was not a safe place.

Jessica pondered what her problem could be. She could not sleep, was wrought with anxiety and could not feel settled about the situation.

Recycling allowed Jessica to look at her childhood and to get some support from friends and professionals. The support Jessica gave her daughter, Lacey as well as the support Jessica received from the caring adults in her life, helped to smooth out the original injury. Because of her awareness of the recycling phenomenon, Jessica sought support to heal her scars from past years. She is a healthier woman today because her child gave her the gift of recycling, a chance to smooth out the pain of her childhood.

Lynn & Carly

Lynn was excited to have a baby. For years she had wanted to experience the mystery of childbirth and caring for a new life. Two years after her marriage, she became pregnant and embarked on her journey.

After baby Carly was born, things began to go wrong. Lynn was surprised by a flood of strange feelings, including feelings of utter incompetence. She loved the baby, but simply could not get breastfeeding situated. She could not sleep and she felt very self-conscious. She wanted to be cared for, but did not have the words to ask for it. Her hopes for a beautiful new family turned sour.

Lynn's family history provides clues to her recycling process. Her mother also loved children and had always wanted a baby. She married a compulsive alcoholic, a man who was undependable and totally unsupportive. The grandparents said they wanted to help in whatever way they could, but her grandmother's cues implied to the new mother, "You made your bed. You sleep in it." Lynn's mother did not ask for or receive care as a new mother.

Baby Lynn was born into a complex family group of adults who had their own needs. One can surmise that Lynn received little— if any—loving gazes as a baby. Lynn was recycling what she had received and seen, which essentially meant: "Don't ask. Suffer."

She needed a lot of affirmation for her own existence—the affirmation she needed many years before as an infant and never got— so that she could affirm and care for her baby. Thanks to recycling, both Jessica and Lynn have a chance to build on their self-esteem and to live healthier lives.

Renewed Emotional Health

The gift of supportive care you receive during your childbearing year can provide for renewed emotional health. A woman who is nurtured and supported during this journey will naturally weigh the old, painful experiences against the new, helpful ones—and many women will choose to absorb the care and begin to feel a sense of well-being.

Recycling seems to indicate that it is never too late to become healthy—to have a happy childhood.

Your Hills and Valleys

Perhaps you now understand why you may not feel that you're thriving during this "wonderful" time in your life. Due to your own unsupported childhood, you may not have a gardening plan for caring for yourself or your child.

"And even though I taught my daughter the opposite,
still she came out the same way!
Maybe it was because she was born to me and she was born a girl.
And I was born to my mother and I was born a girl.
All of us are like stairs, one step after another, going up
and down, but all going the same way."
—AMY TAN, *THE JOY LUCK CLUB*

Discovering the hills and valleys in your meadow can help you learn how to take better care of yourself and better care of your baby. You can learn about nurturing—again, for the first time—by asking for and accepting care, like your baby does. "You can grow up again—get what you missed as a child. It's an opportunity to finally have what you need, so you don't have to go on living without it."[3]

Communication

Because experiences during the childbearing journey form snapshot-like memories that lodge in the brain, it's important for the communication between you and your support team to be positive and helpful.

Research has proven that when a woman on the childbearing journey receives positive strokes, compliments and helpful nurture, her self-esteem is enhanced for a lifetime.

This point cannot be made strongly enough. The memories of positive strokes received during the childbearing year weigh heavier than those received at any other time in your life. Sadly, a negative stroke or unhelpful communication during the childbearing year also weighs heavier than one received at other times of your life. It is critical, then, to plan for helpful strokes when possible and be aware of and resolve any negative communication that takes place.

Reframing Memories

By resolving the communication between you and your support team, you can clear up any misunderstandings and enhance your development as a mother. This reframing process consists of:

- ❀ Learning to understand how people communicate.
- ❀ Determining why communication sometimes goes haywire.
- ❀ Defining methods to clear up unhelpful communication.

The process of exploring your mothering communication garden-path, is like putting a new frame on a valuable, sentimental portrait. You take off the old frame—old patterns of negative communication—and put on a new one—helpful, positive patterns of communication.

Not only does positive communication nurture you through a new and unsure time, it also tends to clear out negative communication from the past.

The Parts of Your Personality

When in the process of resolving negative communication, you need to understand what part of your personality is holding onto and playing back old patterns of communication. As you already know, there are three parts to your personality. Understanding them simplifies the "reframing" process.

The parts of your personality give, receive, replay, evaluate and make decisions about communication. These parts all work together to contribute to the way you communicate. By figuring out how they operate, you may become aware of your own, as well as others', helpful and unhelpful patterns of communication and work cooperatively with key people in your life to recreate them.

To remind you, the three personality parts are: the Parent, the Adult, and the Child.[4] All of these personalities live inside us and pop up to play a part on specific occasions.

THE PARENT behaves and thinks like all the authority figures in your life, including your parents. Your Parent stores information you received from your teachers, grandparents, religious leaders and your parents. It tells you what to do, how to do it and when to do it. It is the part of your personality that stores values and beliefs that guide you in how to be in the world. The Parent is a caretaker. It has stored helpful and unhelpful parenting messages from your past. It has a critical or rigid side as well as a positive side, which holds rules that provide helpful structure.

THE ADULT thinks, analyzes and figures things out in the present. The Adult evaluates the world you live in and decides what you need to do today. When you find yourself examining what's happening—right here, right now, in the present—you are getting a message from your Adult. Your goal is to make sense of and *transmit* messages relevant to the here and now.

THE CHILD functions within a range of emotions and thoughts available to children. Your creative, intuitive side comes from your Child part. It has stored all your beliefs about yourself from your childhood. It remembers both helpful and unhelpful transactions from the past.

Each part of the personality has both a nurturing and a critical aspect. Your Critical Parent, for example, can be destructive—as can your Critical Adult or Critical Child. Your Nurturing Parent, Adult and Child, however, are supportive. Getting acquainted with the parts of your personality can help to:

- Maintain or regain trust in yourself and your support team.
- Evaluate the quality of support offered by the support team and caregivers.
- Connect positive feelings to yourself and to others.

When humans communicate, we generally transmit from one of our three personality parts—Parent, Adult or Child. The person we transmit to receives the information into one of their three parts and may transmit back from a different part.

It is possible then, to be speaking from your Child, to another person who is receiving the information to his Parent. If the information stored and shared in each person's part is positive, the communication transaction is likely to be positive, too. If the information stored is negative, the communication could go haywire.

You can only take in what is available to you. As a child, you naturally took into your personality elements from what your environment provided. What was offered to you was out of your control. As an adult, you can choose to create an environment that is more supportive and rich in emotional security for you and your family.

Every person's memory is capable of transmitting positive communication. Negative information from past transactions result in negative decisions, which then impede the communication.

**You can change your whole life plan,
whenever you decide!**

The birth of your baby is a perfect time to evaluate and rewrite old messages—also to reconnect with your inner abilities, feelings and hopes that may have been lying dormant because of what's been stored in your brain.

The natural recycling that takes place and the proven weight of positive snapshot memories can improve the path of your life. Your baby may be the key that opens the door to a healthier pathway on your journey—both as a woman and as a mother.

> *"Out of the mouths of babes and sucklings
> hast thou ordained strength."*
> —Psalms 8:2

Exploring a Rainbow of Feelings

Typically, we present to the outside world the feelings we have come to believe are most acceptable to the people we live with. These adapted feelings may not be as helpful as they once were. When you were a child you saved information in your Child part that kept you safe in your family unit. This information included which emotions were okay and which were not okay with your family.

Your baby was born with nature's full operating instructions for all human emotions and feelings. The recycling process will stir in you curiosity about emotions previously unavailable to you. You may find it interesting to allow yourself to reconnect, recapture and save these dormant emotions. Look upon the childbearing year as a gift of rediscovery, an important time to become aware of the full range of your emotional capabilities.

As a parent you will experience many situations that will require the most effective emotions. Emotions or feelings are the motivating forces that move us to problem-solve. When your baby moves, for example, toward the stairs, which are unsafe, you need to feel scared so that you move instinctually to protect the baby.

If feeling scared was not acceptable in your family of origin, you may want to reevaluate that rule so that you can be a better parent. Because of your feelings limitation in your upbringing, your family's health and safety may be compromised.

Feelings of anger can help you take action to resolve a difficult situation. Feelings of fear, when you are in danger, can move you to get out of a dangerous situation. Take cues from your child, who is yet to have feelings censored. Decide to reconnect with your abilities to feel all your feelings. They are nature's tools to health and well-being!

When you enable yourself to feel your feelings, you enable your child to feel his or hers as well. Only then can you better evaluate the care you are giving your children.

Recycling Is a Process

The developmental jobs of infants between birth and age six months are to be, to thrive, to trust, to call out to have their needs met, and to be joyful. During this stage of learning it is O.K. to be here, infants take in and accept nurture and unconditional care.

As adults, we may lose this natural knowledge. We might forget that we, too, have to get our needs met regarding our very existence. The "child" inside us wants to be cared for, to be affirmed for "being." Our baby will remind us of this developmental job from our past. We sometimes set things up so that we recreate what is familiar from the past, even if what is familiar is unhelpful. To get our needs met, to enhance our self-esteem and ultimately care for our children so that they grow to be healthy, we must avoid putting ourselves in scenarios that set us up to duplicate any negative care we received from years passed.

As we become aware of our recycling, we need to be patient. When we see all the possibilities of ways to build a healthier family, we may want it all at once. We can take the lead from our babies, who find a place for one piece of the human developmental puzzle at a time.

All humans experience surges in their development. These surges don't progress in a straight uphill line. When your baby is learning to walk, she may take two steps forward, plop down on her rear end, roll over, crawl and then get up and take one step. This is normal for the baby—and for you.

Recycling offers hope and also a chance to experience faith, and the belief in things that are present but are yet to be. Go ahead, grow up again—and again and again!

MY TOOLSHED:
EQUIPMENT TO ENHANCE MY GROWTH & DEVELOPMENT

Considering the Weight of Childbearing Memories

Part 1:

❀ Time yourself to see how long it takes to recall the two events.
❀ Think about events unrelated to childbirth that happened five days ago.
❀ Write down two of them.

Event 1: ....

Event 2: ....

Time: ....

❀ Time yourself to see how long it takes to recall the two events.
❀ Now, think about specific events of becoming a mother.
❀ Write down two of them.

Event 1: ....

Event 2: ....

Time: ....

Which events appear to be emblazoned most strongly in your memory?

Which events can you recall faster?

Which events have stronger emotions tied to them?

Part 2:

Choose one of the memories you have on your list from five days ago that involves a communication, or think of a recent communication. Write your responses to the following:

❀ Think about which part you communicated from—your Parent, your Adult or your Child.

❀ Were you using the words "should" or "could"?
Do you suppose those words came from your Critical Parent or Nurturing Parent?

❀ Did you feel like a child, not being cared for? Or were you thinking clearly about the situation and problem-solving in the here and now?

❀ From which part do you think the other person might have communicated?

❀ Was the communication positive? Was the information you saved helpful?

❀ What were you feeling when you were communicating? What do you think the other person was feeling?

❀ What would you like to change about the communication?

*"The events of childhood do not pass
but repeat themselves like the seasons of the year."*
—ELEANOR FARJEON

MY TOOLSHED:
EQUIPMENT TO ENHANCE MY GROWTH & DEVELOPMENT

Evaluating Labels from Your Past

THE LABELS YOU CARRY and the predictions that were once made about who you are, are from your past and no longer fit today. The naturally cleansing "recycling" that occurs during the child-bearing year gives you an opportunity to evaluate these labels. You are capable of making a decision to trash negative old labels and to stop living through the eyes of other people's predictions. Your baby may be the key that unlocks a door of personal growth for you.

My Baby's Feelings and Needs

❀ Observe how your baby uses his or her pallet of feelings to get deserved, helpful care.

Carrie

Baby Carrie is very uncomfortable and angry about her dirty diaper. She screams loudly to signal that she is uncomfortable and needs someone to care for her. She uses her full range of normal feelings to get help with her diaper.

My Feelings and My Needs

❀ Think about what feelings you display to the world.

❀ Consider the way you present your feelings—are your needs being met?

Kristen

Angry with her husband, Joe, Kristen wants to get things straightened out. She learned as a child to pout, to stuff her mad feelings. She does this with Joe and hopes he will "guess" what is wrong. The way she presents her angry feelings is by pouting.

❀ Can you think of another way Kristen might get her needs met better?

❀ Do you think there may be a more effective way to get *your* needs met?

❀ Evaluate the conclusions you saved in your Child and Parent portions of your personality that may limit your use of certain feelings. Contemplate what feelings would work better for you today to satisfy your needs and the needs of those you care for. Evaluate whether you need to alter the conclusions you came to as a child about particular kinds of feelings.

MY TOOLSHED:
EQUIPMENT TO ENHANCE MY GROWTH & DEVELOPMENT

Growing up Again[5]

Here is a list of clues that may signal you are in the process of recycling the "Being Stage." The clues listed below may indicate you need to do some growing up again:[6]

❀ Have no idea what you need.

❀ Want others to know what you need without your asking.

❀ Don't need anything—feel numb.

❀ Believe others' needs are more important than yours.

❀ Don't trust others to come through for you.

❀ Don't want to be touched, or you compulsively touch.

❀ Are unwilling to disclose information about yourself, especially negative information.

Nurturing Affirmations

On page 145 are some affirmations[7]—lines to adopt and write into your life's play. They are designed to affirm the being stage of development, for you and your baby. They will also support your partner and the new grandparents, who may be recycling too. The birth is likely to support recycling this being stage in any adult connected with the birth of the baby.

145

Say these affirmations to yourself and to your baby five times in the morning, five times at bedtime or anytime you need to feel nurtured or affirmed for being.

❀ I'm glad you are alive.

❀ You belong here.

❀ What you need is important to me.

❀ I'm glad you are you.

❀ You can grow at your own pace.

❀ You can feel all your feelings.

❀ I love you and care for you.

As you begin to become aware of your own recycling, attempt to stay "underwhelmed." When we see all the possibilities of ways to build a healthier family, we may want it all at once. Take the lead from your baby who practices one at a time the skills of the human developmental puzzle. You and your baby have permission to grow at your own pace, to fill in pieces of your development a little at a time.

All humans experience surges in their development. These surges don't progress in a straight uphill line. The blocks of development get scattered and are restacked at each phase of growth. Your baby will take two steps forward then, plop down on his rear end, roll over, crawl and then maybe get up and take one step. This is normal for the baby and for you, to take one step at a time. Acquiring new skills and reshaping old skills takes time . . . it is time well spent. Recycling offers hope, it also offers a chance to experience faith and the belief in things that are present but are yet to be.

"Growing up again is a process,
not a onetime accomplishment."
—JEAN ILLSLEY CLARKE AND CONNIE DAWSON
GROWING UP AGAIN, PARENTING OURSELVES, PARENTING OUR CHILDREN

MY JOURNAL:
TURNING OVER A NEW LEAF OF DISCOVERY

Rewriting Messages

YOUR SELF-ESTEEM CAN IMPROVE during the childbearing year. By storing helpful communications and evaluating unhelpful ones from yourself and others, you can improve the quality and impressions of memories and enhance your self-image.

❀ Write in your journal a communication that was not helpful to you in the last few days.

❀ Rewrite the message! Write it the way you want to hear it!

❀ Write in your journal a helpful communication you remember receiving in the last several days.

❀ Write what it means to you.

❀ Does it remind you of anything from your past? What specifically?

❀ Challenge archaic, antiquated messages from the past and replace them with sensible ideas for today. Understand that they are old and may have no further meaning in your life now.

❀ Look at the following quotation and write in your journal what it means to you.

> *"If a child lives with approval,*
> *he learns to live with himself."*
> —DOROTHY LAW NOLTE

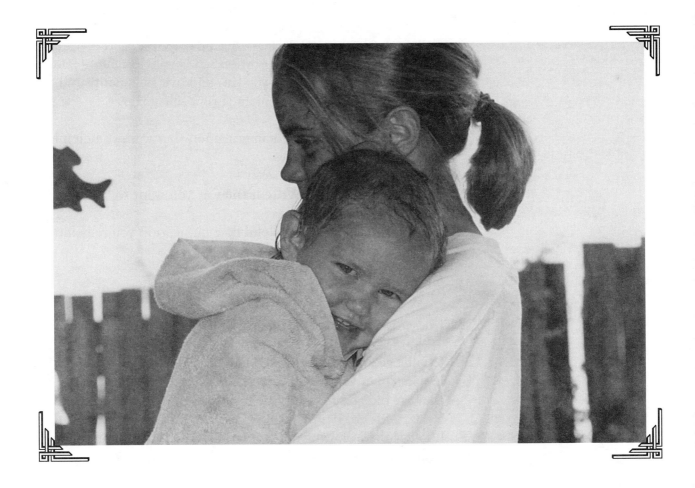

CHAPTER 8

Reaping an Emotionally Secure Family

*"There is always one moment in childhood
when the door opens and lets the future in."*
—GRAHAM GREENE,
THE POWER AND THE GLORY

When a woman becomes a mother, she brings many skills she learned from her childhood family—her family of origin. Sometimes these skills are helpful, and sometimes they're not.

No matter what skills you have learned, the beauty of building a new family group is that you can:

❀ Choose to keep the skills that are supportive.
❀ Evaluate the ones that are not supportive.
❀ Adopt new skills to plant in your family-garden.

Foundation Tools

All human beings deserve to live in homes that support them. When adults and children live with a sense of emotional security, their natural talents are allowed to thrive and expand. With a few foundation tools, you can support your new garden (plants) as it emerges into a healthy reality.

Tool #1: House Rules[1]

Posting house rules lets all family members know what expectations they need to abide by for the mutual benefit—nurture and structure—of all household members. This means that the family has established a set of group behaviors expected of all members.

Because mothers and fathers have had experiences of living in another family unit—the family group they came from—and because the care they received in their original family unit can affect the relationships of the new family they are building, house rules can help keep the new family group on a balanced and defined path.

Keeping your house rules to a minimum ensures that everyone will remember what they are. When designing house rules for your family, consider the following:

❀ **Leave Room for Flexibility**
As the family grows and needs change, the rules need to be flexible enough to grow and change with them. Insisting, for example, that all family members be in bed by 8:00 p.m. when the youngest family member is 12 years old may not suit the needs of the group.

❀ **Make Family Meetings a Habit**

Have regular family meetings to discuss rules. Starting this process when your child is an infant will set a precedent. If there are concerns that abuse or neglect an adult suffered as a child may affect the new family, discuss these issues early to help build a healthy foundation.

❀ **Post Rules Where All Family Members Can See Them**

Post the agreed-upon rules in plain sight. Later, when the children are older, the posted house rules will serve as "enforcer" so that you no longer have to play that role. They instill values you wish early in the journey, so that they become a natural part of an established family order.

See "My Toolshed: Equipment to Enhance My Growth and Development" on page 163 for sample house rules for postpartum families.

Tool #2: Affirmations

Nurturing affirmations[2] can support the normal growing stages of children and the recycling of adults. These affirmations are barebones statements that speak to the child-side of you, offering you nurture and structure.

Most of us grow up with what Jean Illsley Clarke and Connie Dawson call "uneven parenting"—the hills and valleys of care we receive as children. Affirmations can support our mothering journey and the journey of building an emotionally secure family. They actualize the words we needed to hear as a child and can offer our babies now. On page 145 you can find some affirmations for this stage of your family's development.

Many crises may be avoided by becoming aware of a family member's tendency toward perfectionism and using "black-or-white" thinking—that is, believing that something is either right or wrong, true or false, black or white.

Some people see the world as a polarized place—that is, a place where everything is all one way or all another. They believe something or someone is either good or bad, strong or weak, hot or cold. "Black-or-white" thinking shows no respect for another person's frame of reference and adopted belief position and does not appreciate that person's efforts to function in a way that makes sense to her or to him in that moment.

**One sure indicator of an impending crisis
is a family member insisting upon perfection.
While most of us have the highest goals and the best intentions,
all human beings fail from time to time.**

While understandable, perfectionism does not serve new parents. For example, black-or-white thinking frequently rears its head when it comes to such matters as breastfeeding. Some people believe, without exception, that all babies should be breastfed and that all good mommies should breastfeed. In reality there are many good methods of feeding. Black-or-white thinking uses absolute or global words such as: "always," "should," "never," "good" and "bad."

Emotionally secure families, however, learn that in the family, as well as in life in general, there are many shades of gray. What works for one family may not work for another, but the best rules for avoiding crisis are:

❀ Ask for and receive supportive care.
❀ Learn the signals of an upcoming crisis.
❀ Learn appropriate structure and boundaries for managing crisis.

By adopting a rule of mutual respect, a family can appreciate all efforts that are made, choose new directions, and refocus their path, knowing at all times that they are doing the best they can with the tools they have in that moment.

"When you eliminate the idea of perfection,
nothing can hold you back—you loose your fear."
—ALEXANDRA STODDARD

Tool #4: Family Covenant

The family covenant is a written vow in which family members promise to care for each other in a healthy way. For adults who have been abused, the family covenant is a promise to not abuse children in any way and to learn helpful parenting skills.

All of us need a home, a place that will love and nurture us. You and the father of your baby need to receive regular doses of loving hugs, kisses, words and deeds to share with your baby. The Family Covenant is a promise to provide positive ways to care for one another.

See "My Toolshed: Equipment to Enhance My Growth and Development" on pages 164 & 165 for a sample family covenant as well as a covenant for caring for your children.

Tool #5: Creating Contracts for Change

The use of a contract with family members during the childbearing year can be supportive to the goals of each member. So often in families, people have good intentions of behaving in a certain manner or completing a certain task that was mutually agreed upon; but, for some reason, promises go unfulfilled or take a form that's different from what was originally planned.

When well-laid plans do not come to fruition, there can be negative feelings. These feeling can grind on the emotional security of the family and cause negative results.

A contract for change provides an agreed-upon starting point and tends to help keep people on track. Such a contract need not be used as punishment, but rather a logical agreement between individuals who care for each other and have similar goals and desires. They are most helpful if all individuals involved are required to play a role in ensuring that the contract is fulfilled. Both a reward for completing the contract and consequences for not abiding by the contract need to be outlined ahead of time.

When goals or decisions are written down, they are more likely to become reality. One theory about this phenomenon is that when a person couples his or her thinking with physical movements required to write that thought down, something takes place in the brain that makes the idea more concrete.

All thriving businesses make contracts with their employees. The agreements are documented and steps to be accomplished are outlined. The use of contracts at home may increase the chance that support and nurture will happen. Using a contract helps to keep people on their honor and formalizes the promises and agreements made.

To put together your own contract, use the following format designed by Jean Illsley Clarke and Connie Dawson in *Growing Up Again, Parenting Ourselves, Parenting Our Children:*[3]

❀ What is the mutually agreed-upon goal?

❀ What is currently happening?

❀ What is the desired change—situation or behavior?

❀ How does the proposed activity benefit everyone?

❀ What efforts/actions need to be taken—by whom? When? Where? For how long?

❀ What support has been solicitied? From whom?

❀ If our contract is fulfilled by everyone, what is the positive consequence? What will we celebrate and what will be our rewards?

❀ If our contract is not fulfilled by everyone, what are the negative consequences?

Tool #6: The Blessing Way[4]

Emotionally secure families offer blessings as signs of approval and acceptance into the family group. Blessings are simple ways of ensuring a feeling of emotional security with members of the family.

A blessing is a sign of ultimate acceptance on the part of an elder member of a family to a younger son or daughter. This sign of approval helps children form life-long roots that lead to accep-

The Elements of a Blessing[5]

A Blessing includes all of the following offered together:

❊ **A Meaningful Touch**—A hug, a kiss, laying one's hand on a person can communicate affirmation, warmth and acceptance.

❊ **A Spoken Message**—A blessing can come only when words are spoken. Without them, confusion takes place. People are left to guess what the sender of the blessing might mean. When someone takes the time to say thoughtful words, the person who receives them may then feel worthy of such an honor.

❊ **Attaching High Value**—The blessing demonstrates value based not on what a person does, but on who a person is. Using metaphors or picture words helps the person see the picture of deep value you intend. These picture words can also illustrate the potential of the person.
  • **Example:** "Elisabeth, you are like the rising sun— bright, warm and glowing."
  • **Example:** "Elisabeth, you are like the hawk, capable of soaring to great heights and traveling remarkable distances in the journey of life."

❊ **Picturing the Future**—This encourages a person to seek future goals.
  • **Example:** "Elisabeth, when I think of you as an adult, I see someone who has found meaningful relationships and ways to make your world a better place to live." Beware of expectations with unattainable goals. The goal is to help the person accept herself with confidence for the future.

❊ **An Active Commitment**—This is a commitment to do everything possible to help the blessed be successful.
  • **Example:** "Elisabeth, I will assist you in any way I can to ensure that you grow up to be the best person possible."

tance of themselves in their community. Centuries old, this tradition dates back to Old Testament times, when a blessing was a momentous sign of parents' deep value of their children.

A new mother needs to receive an ultimate feeling of acceptance—as a human being, a woman, a daughter and a mother. A blessing can provide a much needed welcome mat of approval that can inspire her to greater heights in her new role. That's why this idea can be very valuable during the childbearing year.

Offering the spiritual connection of a blessing to key people in your life can help to satisfy deep emotional needs of acceptance for yourself and them.

> *"Provide a flower with the essential elements it needs,*
> *and watch it grow!"*
> —GARY SMALLEY AND JOHN TRENT, *THE BLESSING*

Spreading Emotional Health

It has been said that when one member of a family group begins to live in a healthier, more supportive fashion, other members of the family feel the effects that may result in a positive change for them, too. The process of healing is like throwing a rock into a pool—the ripples you make by creating change touch your family members, who will feel the benefits brought on by your emotional security.

As you choose to live a more healthful life, your family may reach for the same experiences for themselves. They may also choose to stay as they are, feeling the ripples, but not moving to a healthier spot.

Either way there is an effect. You deserve emotional security and so does your baby. It is not your responsibility to claim emotional security for the whole extended family. As family members watch you model emotional security, regardless of whether they decide to jump in or not, their lives will never be the same.

Beware of the tendency to want to save others in your group. The birth of a baby is life's renewal time for families—an opportunity to evaluate how emotionally secure that family has been. Regardless of the decisions of your family members, your choices of emotional security are important.

❀ Spend time caring for yourself.
❀ Lead by example.
❀ Stay in the present as you forge forward to a life of emotional security.
❀ Start slowly and add pieces as they fit.

Components of an Emotionally Secure Family

Emotionally secure families:

❀ Guarantee that the family group is dedicated to care and nurture the well-being of the family's individuals as well as the group.

❀ Provide a place where adults and children can live with abundant, unconditional love, which is love offered without a price tag—given freely without strings.

❀ Build the self-esteem of each member by affirming each person for who she or he is as well as what each can do. They take pride in the individual uniqueness of their members; they highlight and appreciate the gifts of each person. The group supports each person becoming all he/she can be.

❀ Learn about the developmental stages of their children. They are aware of what can be expected of the children at each stage and avoid pushing children to do things that are beyond their developmental stage.

❀ Avoid keeping the children small and provide children with many opportunities to practice their skills.

❀ Have a belief system with values that are conveyed to each of the members. The belief system and values provide a purpose for the lives of each member of the family.

❀ Develop a thirst for knowledge and constantly seek other families and adults in order to spend time and share information.

MY TOOLSHED:
EQUIPMENT TO ENHANCE MY GROWTH & DEVELOPMENT

I. Positive and Negative Strokes—
Avoiding Crisis

"I get so stressed being cooped up with the baby.
I want to talk to my husband about the way I feel,
but I seem to pick a fight instead."
—A YAKIMA DISCOVERY GROUP PARTICIPANT

"Family faces are magic mirrors.
Looking at people who belong to us
we see the past, present and future."
—GAIL LUMET BUCKLEY

THE ONLY WAY SOME PEOPLE have received attention is by getting negative strokes. Some people believe that strokes come only when there's a crisis to create and solve. By having watched others get strokes only in a crisis, possibly during episodes of domestic violence or disputes, a conclusion may have been drawn. These individuals may have decided that this is the only way to get attention.

Crisis can be real or imagined, meaning that something could have really happened that was traumatic. In this case those who helped to solve the problem may have received strokes for their efforts.

Because human beings need strokes to thrive, one can understand that any stroke—even a negative one—is better that no stroke at all. The question is: Do these people—do you—want to continue living this way, or would they or you prefer a more positive lifestyle?

Sometimes it's difficult to say what we're really thinking or feeling. Because of our past history, we may fear speaking the truth. What we'll do instead is say something to cover up the truth—like the front of a candy store covering elicit activities in the back room.

Be aware of storefront feelings that hide what's really going on inside you. People sometimes use these feelings as ways to increase their strokes or connect with a family member by starting a fight and getting a negative stroke, rather than asking straight for the stroke they need.

Jane & Bob

Jane and Bob were on their way to visit relatives in California. They spent a day preparing for the trip. When they got to the airport they discovered that the flight had been canceled. On the drive back to their house they started picking at each other.

"Did you get the diapers for the baby?" asked Bob.

"I thought *you* were going to get them! By the way, did you lock the front door?" said Jane.

Neither of them said a word about their anger with the airline for canceling the flight. They created a crisis on other issues to avoid the real one. Rather than stating the obvious, they used a storefront feeling to disguise what was really troubling them.

II. Crisis Connections—Ways to Get Out

❀ Write what you did for the day as a way to connect with someone in your family. Make plans to talk about the day rather than start a fight to get attention. Say to that person, "I want to share with you what happened in my day and I would like to hear about your day too. Are you willing to spend time with me talking about the day now or later on tonight?"

❀ Reprioritize your thinking and lower your expectations of yourself and your family member. So often the expectations we have about relationships are out of line and unrealistic. Let your feelings be known by writing them down or drawing a picture.

❀ Because there are no visible products, many family members fail to acknowledge all the work that goes into caring for an infant during the course of a day. Ask them to notice and comment.

❀ Design a signal to indicate to a family member that you are going into crisis. You might say, "I'm feeling like there is something negative going on, and I need your help to sort through this. Will you help me out?" Ask a family member to observe you when a crisis happens and report back to you any obvious patterns. Agree together that pointing these behaviors out to head off a potential crisis is a positive step.

❀ Define for yourself the physical signals just prior to a crisis. You may be able to head it off by isolating your physical signals and thinking about ways to avoid starting a fight.

❀ Switch channels and smile. New research indicates that humans can actually tap into the good-feeling, positive hormone, adrenaline, by smiling. Next time you feel like finding a crisis, smile and see what happens.

❀ Don't bottle up feelings. Some people will collect negative feelings and unload them on others. This is guaranteed to create emotional commotion. Talk soon!

❀ Start seeing yourself as the lovable, capable person you are. See how many ways you can collect positive strokes just for being who you are.

III. Sample House Rules for Postpartum Families

❀ Treat each person with mutual respect, honoring individual differences.

❀ Ask for care and help simply and forthrightly.

❀ Discuss feelings to reduce tension and strengthen communication.

❀ Work together to maintain the house.

MY TOOLSHED:
EQUIPMENT TO
ENHANCE MY
GROWTH &
DEVELOPMENT

Our Family Covenant

We _____

on this _____ day of _____ in the year _____ , promise to care for one another and that we will:

❀ Be dedicated to the care and nurture of our own well-being as well as the well-being of the group.

❀ Provide a place where adults can live with abundant, unconditional love, offered with no price tag, given freely with no strings.

❀ Take pride in how we care for each other and will ensure that no one has to go without care for the sake of another person.

❀ Celebrate and thrive on our unity and help each individual feel secure by providing a sense of belonging.

❀ See ourselves and other family members as lovable for who we are as well as what we can do.

❀ Use humor in helpful ways and convey our beliefs to each of the members. Our shared beliefs and values will provide a purpose for our lives.

❀ Constantly work on the flow of communication and look for improved ways of communicating.

❀ Accept the wide rainbow of feelings available to human beings and learn ways to express feelings in helpful ways.

❀ Dedicate ourselves to resolving conflict in healthy ways.

❀ We will avoid actions that lead to the loss of trust in the group and understand the benefit of asking for and giving forgiveness.

A Covenant for Caring for Our Children

We promise that we will:

❀ Take time to get to know you, learn who you are and do our best to avoid trying to make you fit into our prescribed beliefs about who you might be. We will talk with you and listen to you.

❀ Acknowledge your individual temperament style, answer your cries and requests for help and realize when you cry that you are communicating rather than trying to control us.

❀ Feed you when you are hungry, pick you up and hold you, understanding how important holding you is for your healthy development.

❀ Take care of ourselves so that we can take better care of you.

❀ When we feel angry, we will put you in a safe place, like your crib. Ask for help from someone else while we will leave the area to calm down. We will seek support in learning to use anger in helpful ways.

❀ Seek help when we run out of energy or solutions to problems, and information on current helpful ways to raise children. We will monitor the effects of our parenting you.

❀ Seek help, if we were sexually abused, to heal from the confusing hurtful past we may have experienced as children.

❀ Keep you safe by using appropriate safety equipment such as a carseat and safety gates.

❀ Celebrate your development and offer you verbal and written affirmations for your growth.

❀ We will not expect you to be perfect, but offer support as you grow and help you learn from your experiences.

MY TOOLSHED:
EQUIPMENT TO ENHANCE MY GROWTH & DEVELOPMENT

The Importance of Touch

ALL HUMAN BEINGS NEED TO BE TOUCHED in order to grow and thrive. Babies who are not touched will die. Research has been published suggesting you cannot spoil a baby by picking up the baby. The opposite is actually true. The child will "spoil" if it is not touched.

Some babies simply cry more. Your baby may be telling you, in her own language, that she has had enough stimulation. You may not see the signs because you simply don't know them. Train yourself to watch for these cues so your baby may not have to get to a full cry to tell you when he's had enough. You might try writing down the various cues you baby uses to help you remember.

New mothers need to be hugged, cuddled, snuggled and touched, too, in order to know how to do this for their babies. There are many ways for new mothers to get their touching needs met.

Touches for Mom and Baby

❀ **Massage.** Full body, back or even simply foot or hand massage. This can be done by a massage therapist or you can borrow a book on massage from the library or a friend, or buy one from your local bookseller and learn how to do it yourself.

❀ **Rocking.** Lie on a bed and have a support person rock your body by moving it back and forth, swaying from side to side. You can also enjoy a rocking chair. The rocking motion serves as a comforting form of touch that feels gentle and soothing.

❀ **Hammock.** Purchase or borrow a hammock to use by yourself or with another person. The tight secure cradling of the hammock will duplicate the tight cozy feeling of being swaddled, which helps both infants and mothers feel secure.

❀ **Bath.** Have someone give you a bath. Ask her/him to wash your back, your neck, your arms and feet. Soak in the water and let it support your body. Let your worries drift away as you feel refreshed and clean.

❀ **Hug.** Ask for a long, nurturing hug—the kind in which you keep embracing until you melt into the other person's arms. Practice feeling the warm glow offered when two people hug for a long time.

❀ **The Sling.** Babies are used to the cramped quarters of the womb, where their activities occur in a limited physical environment. The sling that you wear on your body duplicates this environment and helps to organize the baby's physical movements, making the baby feel comfortable. Here are some benefits of baby wearing:

• Enhances learning because the baby can see everything.

• Socializes the baby by letting the little one observe how humans act.

• Promotes extended bond between the baby and family members. The baby is part of the function of the family and sibling can wear the baby.

• Allows parents to have both of their hands free.

• Helps babies learn language because they are better able to see and hear how words are formed.

• Offers the caregiver a chance to keep an eye on the baby; keeps the baby comfortable and more regulated.

• Offers a caregiver the chance to anticipate the needs of the baby and offer comfort before the baby has to signal dramatically through crying that he/she needs something. This can reduce amount and intensity of crying.

Securing Safety When Feeling Angry, Mad, Frustrated and You Are Alone and Can't Get Help With the Baby.

When you feel angry and suspect you are are at risk for hurting the baby, do the following steps recommended by Patty Mould, MSW, who teaches a parenting class on anger.

Step 1. PUT THE BABY DOWN—IMMEDIATELY!
(in a safe place, on the floor if she is not crawling, in a playpen or in the crib).

Step 2.

❀ *Exit.* Remove yourself from where the baby is. Do not return to touch the baby until you have completed the following steps. Do not shake your baby, which can cause brain damage, blindness or even death! Shut the door and go outside.

❀ *Remove Yourself.* This gives you time to calm down and to think.

❀ Do not return until the intensity of your feelings has diminished.

Once you can, say to your baby, "I've done all I know how to do, I am feeling angry and I need a moment to myself. I'm going to put you in your crib, and I will be back to check on you when I feel less (fill in the blank with what you are feeling.)"

Step 3. Do something to release the strong feeling.

❀ *The Tarzan Yell.* Especially helpful for extraverts, yell to release pent-up energy. Let it all out!

❀ *Sit Quietly.* Sit as peacefully as you can, away from the baby, possibly outside or in your car, or go next door to a neighbor's house for a few minutes, until you can think.

❀ *Breathe Deeply.* Use deep chest breathing you may have learned in childbirth class.

❀ *Get Physical.* Take a walk outside, or walk around your house. Physical exertion helps to dissipate strong feelings.

Step 4. Think. When you feel a change in the intensity of your feelings, begin to think about what triggered your anger. Write it down if you know what it is or call a friend to listen to you and help determine what the trigger is. Ask yourself, "What do you think the problem is?"

Step 5. Evaluate and create new ways to feel your anger. For example, recognize your anger as a sign that you need help or need to solve a problem. Anger itself is not bad; negative reactions to anger are what is unhelpful.

Step 6. Other ideas:

❀ Tell yourself to stop!

❀ Call for help.

❀ Take a nap.

❀ Schedule regular walks to relieve stress.

❀ Avoid being isolated, get out of the house frequently.

❀ Contract for regular breaks from your baby each day.

❀ Get a copy of *Meditations for the New Mother* and read it.

❀ Do necessary household tasks early to avoid additional stress.

❀ Turn up the music; dance and sing at the top of your lungs.

❀ Take the phone off the hook to avoid unwanted disturbances.

❀ Keep track of the times you feel stress and trigger points.

❀ Remember you are not alone.

❀ Adjust your expectations.

❀ Concentrate on an inspirational verse or music lyric.

❀ Remind yourself of what you love about your baby.

❀ Think of something funny.

❀ Give yourself a reward to look forward to after a long day of infant care.

❀ Use ear plugs to reduce how loud the crying sounds.

MY JOURNAL:
TURNING OVER A NEW LEAF OF DISCOVERY

 Express Yourself

❀ Write any "storefront" feelings you put out into the world.

❀ Write the real feelings behind them.

❀ How many ways can you collect positive strokes for just being who you are?

❀ Name one childbearing memory you have reframed since reading this book.

❀ If you had to describe your rainbow of feelings, what would you say?

❀ Name one way you renewed your emotional health this week.

❀ What's your favorite affirmation?

CHAPTER 9

A Garden of Detours
& New Landscape Plans

*"Fortunately for children,
the uncertainties of the present always give way
to the enchanted possibilities of the future."*
—GELSEY KIRKLAND

As you experience your childbearing journey, the detours will be many and they will sometimes try your patience and stability, but you have the exciting opportunity to learn new skills and ideas to enhance your life. The path may not be easy, but the choice is always yours.

In this chapter you will find detours in the following categories:

❀ Pregnancy
❀ Labor and Delivery
❀ Postpartum
❀ Baby

Pregnancy Detours

The dramatic levels of hormones produced by your body to maintain the pregnancy can have a major effect on your body, mind and spirit. As you read through these, honor who you are and let this information help you.

Unexpected Pregnancy

"When I first found out I was pregnant, I was scared, nervous, excited, mad and happy. I didn't know what to do. My family was 2-1/2 hours away from me and I felt very alone. I wasn't sure if I wanted to give everything up. I saw my dreams slip out of reach."

"I always thought I would be a mother. In my dreams I wanted two children—a boy and a girl. When I met my husband we talked about children, and he said he never wanted to become a parent. He revealed that he never thought of himself in that way and would do everything to prevent it. I guess we are the 1% birth-control failure. I ended up pregnant. He is slowly accepting it, but it sure seems like a long road."

> *"To every thing there is a season,*
> *and a time to every purpose under the heaven . . ."*
> —ECCLESIASTES 3:1

❀ It is never appropriate to blame the baby for coming into your life.

❀ Rather than feeling guilty about not wanting to be pregnant, find a safe person who's willing to share your feelings.

❋ Set some adjustment/acceptance goals. Say to yourself, "In two weeks I will have accepted that (fill in the blank) is not a possibility for my life right now." Then, within two weeks, let the issue go.

❋ Keep a list of the things you wish to do in your life. Put it in a file labeled: "Things to Do Later in Life." There is time in life for many dreams.

❋ Revel in the connection with your baby. See where it leads. Your dreams are not abandoned. Some are on hold; others may just be beginning.

❋ Think of the numerous ways you have learned to deal with the unexpected. Start a résumé and add them.

Miscarriage

"After two miscarriages and three and one-half years of being unable to get pregnant I was very apprehensive when I found I was pregnant for a third time. Six weeks into my pregnancy I started spotting and I was put on bedrest. The spotting continued all through the first trimester. I was on an emotional roller coaster—trying to accept the possibility of a miscarriage and then getting my hopes up when things improved. It was awful. An ultrasound showed the baby was growing just fine, the spotting stopped, and I began to relax a bit. Everytime I had a twinge or unusual feeling, fear would grip me and I would worry that something was wrong."

—A YAKIMA DISCOVERY GROUP PARTICIPANT

"I am an old man and have known a great many troubles,
but most of them have never happened."

—MARK TWAIN

If your child was lost due to miscarriage:

❀ Grieve the loss of that baby. Know that no matter how far along they are in their pregnancies, many women imagine themselves with a child and begin to accept the thought of an infant in their lives. When a pregnancy is lost, a woman needs to grieve that loss.

❀ Practice believing the baby you have now, your newborn, is not going to leave. Many women who have experienced miscarriages may reserve themselves emotionally with their pregnancy and then with the subsequent baby, in fear that history will repeat itself. If you find it necessary to hold back, do so. But know that it is more helpful to connect and bond with this pregnancy, then later with your new baby, and to practice loving yourself and the baby in the process.

❀ See yourself as deserving! Women who've had miscarriages sometimes believe they did something to cause the miscarriage. Some believe they are being punished for past mistakes. This is simply not true.

An Unsupportive Father

"I guess I was the one who wanted to have a baby. He went along with it, I mean getting pregnant, but now that she's here, the reality is that he sees this as my job. I can't get him to help with her care, not to mention around the house. What is worst, he is not affirming me as a wife, mother or woman!"
—A YAKIMA DISCOVERY GROUP PARTICIPANT

"My day-old son is plenty scrawny,
His mouth is wide and screams or yawny,
His ears seem larger than his needing.

> *His nose is flat, his chin receding,*
> *His skin is very, very red,*
> *He has no hair upon his head,*
> *And yet I'm proud as proud can be*
> *To hear you say he looks like me."*
> —RICHARD ARMOUR

During Pregnancy

❀ Remember he did not have the physiological benefits of the baby. He did not experience the nausea, the heartburn, the extra weight, the labor or the postpartum hormones. Know that just because a person observes another person going through an experience does not mean that they understand it or know how to help in the process.

❀ Clearly state what support means to you. Ask yourself what you want him to do. Tell him!

❀ Adopt a belief that all members of the family do not have to demonstrate support in the same way.

❀ Consider the hectic schedule of the time . . . pregnancy . . . birth . . . and new parenting. The hurried pace may have diminished your sense of support from your partner.

❀ Don't expect him to be joyful and excited all the time about the pregnancy. He may not have ever imagined himself as a parent or he may have wished to become a parent later— or sooner. Offer him the gift of loving time.

❀ It is normal for a man to grieve the changes in his life he enjoyed prior to pregnancy.

❀ Invite friends who have babies to come over and talk about the gains and the losses. You might see if arranging time alone with other expectant fathers might feel good to him.

❀ Becoming a parent is a process of acceptance for all members of the family. Every day another step or two is taken to adjust to the idea.

Baby Care

❀ No one went to college to learn how to care for a baby, meaning no one needs to pass a test. Let your husband find his own style of caring for the baby. Respect that there are at least 20 ways to take care of a child and that all can be right and fit the situation.

❀ Allow him time and space to find his own way. This may mean leaving him with the baby and going somewhere else so that they can discover their own way of connecting.

❀ Avoid feeling responsible for the relationship between the baby and the baby's father. Remember that he was there too when the baby was conceived. He has responsibilities to connect with this baby and offer support. He is in charge of his relationship with his child.

❀ Inform him that the differences between the way a father and mother treat the baby are important for the baby's development, and that his influences help to break up the boredom and stresses of the day.

❀ Reassure him that it is normal for the baby to want to be with mother because of the close connection experienced in-utero. Babies become familiar with their mother's voice and often prefer her to other people.

❀ The baby may not know the difference in the ways each of you take care of him, after all it is the baby's first time around too.

Breastfeeding

❀ Some men feel jealous of the attention the baby gets during the feedings, and others may not have accepted the fact that a breast can be a way to feed a baby. Talk to him!

❀ Consider that he may be aware of issues related to breastfeeding that you don't see. Take the time to listen to his ideas, write them down and calmly discuss each point.

❀ Ask him if he is dissolutioned with breastfeeding and is interested in feeding the baby as a way to connect with the infant. If so, consider ways that he can be involved in the feeding. Some women will express their breast milk and put it in a bottle so that others, especially dad, can feed the baby (after age six weeks).

Our Relationship

❀ Be aware of any trend toward pulling away from your husband under the guise of caring for the baby. Make a personal commitment to spend time focusing on him too. Simple tasks such as putting a note in his lunch box, calling him for a brief conversation at work, offering a foot massage or picking up his favorite magazine at your next trip to the store may help.

❀ Things have a way of working out through commitment and communication. Encourage him to talk and ask for what he needs.

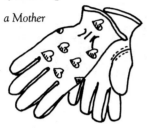

❀ He may be disappearing in the fog of work to avoid intimacy and connection and may believe that he does not deserve the deep potential for love that can come from being a father.

❀ Contract with another adult you trust to care for the baby in a nearby area while you and your partner have time alone. Even half an hour can rejuvenate your marriage connection.

Sexuality

❀ Most physicians recommend waiting six weeks to resume your sexual relationship. Many women believe it takes longer than six weeks to feel confident and comfortable in having sex. Talk to him!

Feelings of Illness

"When I became pregnant with my third child, everything was different. The way I felt about the pregnancy, the event of the pregnancy and the way people treated me. I was more tired and had little energy for the other children, my work or my husband. I felt big and dumpy. And I was nauseous. Then, overnight my body traded nausea and vomiting for heartburn, indigestion and extreme flatulence that lasted from the fifth month to the birth. Thank the Lord for Tums!"

—A YAKIMA DISCOVERY GROUP PARTICIPANT

"My mother had a great deal of trouble with me,
but I think she enjoyed it."
—MARK TWAIN

❀ You have every right to fuss about the inconvenience of the ill feelings caused by pregnancy.

❃ Accurately identify the source of your discomfort, which is the pregnancy, not the baby!

❃ Give yourself credit for how you withstand the discomfort. Many professionals say pregnancy is a normal life experience, but for some women, ill pregnancy feelings do not resemble anything near normal.

❃ Check out a book on pregnancy with anatomy illustrations to give you a visual representation of how your growing uterus affects your entire body.

Pregnancies Vary

"When I became pregnant with my third child, everything was different. The way I felt about pregnancy, the event of the pregnancy and the way people treated me. Friends who knew me would say, "Oh you are going for a boy, hope it works out." This idea could not be farther from my mind! I was more tired and had little energy for the other children, my work, or my husband. My image of myself was different too, I felt big and dumpy."
—A YAKIMA DISCOVERY GROUP PARTICIPANT

"Preserve the old but know the new."
—CHINESE PROVERB

While professionals would like to describe pregnancy in a nice, neat capsule, the truth is that pregnancies vary, even for the same woman. While each pregnancy is different, in reality nothing concrete causes the differences. Such circumstances are varied and often unexplainable.

❀ Practice not comparing your pregnancies and not comparing your children. See each child as the individual he or she is and focus on the ways you have coped with the differences.

❀ Chart for yourself all the differences. Honor the experiences you went through. You grew and changed from them.

❀ Talk to other second- or third-time mothers to discover their differences.

❀ Reframe the pregnancies by considering new skills and other benefits you have gained from the experience. Absorb the positive experiences and find ways to reframe the negative aspects.

Health Concerns

"I am really concerned about my health and the health of my baby. I have had spotting that was concerning and one test came back abnormal. We do not have a family history of these kinds of things and I am frightened."

—A YAKIMA DISCOVERY GROUP PARTICIPANT

"A Gem is not polished without friction nor is a being realized without trials."
—CHINESE PROVERB

❀ Learn to accept the things you cannot change. Find a rainbow of grace that you may be receiving as a result of the experience. Ask yourself whether you have reasonable expectations about your pregnancy. Keep things simple.

❀ Use your doctor as a resource to reassure and dispel any worries you have. If you need additional information on special conditions that run in your family, ask your doctor to copy some research papers on the subject.

❀ Visualize that you are growing a *healthy* baby.

❀ Talk to a genetic counselor and get the statistics regarding any condition you are concerned about. Ask your doctor about doing an ultrasound.

Doctor/Mother-to-Be Relationship

"Everyone told me I would fall in love with my OB/GYN. I didn't. He gave me excellent care, but I didn't feel close to him."
—A YAKIMA DISCOVERY GROUP PARTICIPANT

"We are more interested in making others believe we are happy than in trying to be happy ourselves."
—DUC DE LA ROCHEFOUCAULD-LIANCOURT

❀ Many women mistakenly believe there should be some magical, deeply spiritual patient-physician connection. You do not need a deep relationship to have a positive birth outcome.

❀ If you have an issue with your doctor, determine whether it is an issue of competency or a personality clash.

❀ Practice confronting authority figures such as physicians with your specific concerns. You are a consumer, and you are paying this person to provide a service. Think about how you might behave if you were concerned about your car mechanic's competence.

❀ If the doctor has been unhelpful, and you are concerned that the outcome of the delivery hinges on what you are experiencing, consider talking to him or her about what you are observing. When talking to the doctor, try using this communication:

- When (fill in the blank; describe the incident) happens . . .
- I feel (state clearly how you feel) . . .
- Because (state any factual information).
- So, I'd rather you please do this instead:
  (Tell the doctor what to do).

❀ If the situation is unreconcilable, ask other women for a referral to a different physician.

❀ If the doctor is a male (or a female), consider whether there is something from your emotional past that you are projecting onto this relationship. If this applies to you, seek counseling.

❀ If the problem is with the doctor's employees, consider communicating with them directly or talk to the doctor about how you've been treated.

Labor & Delivery Detours

The Trials of Labor—Perceptions of Pain

"The pain in labor was so amazingly powerful—I can remember asking for pain medication but it was too late; my labor had progressed to a point where the medication was not safe for the baby. I had to deliver naturally when I had planned for some pain relief."

—A YAKIMA DISCOVERY GROUP PARTICIPANT

"You gain strength, courage and confidence by every experience in which you really stop to look fear in the face. You are able to say to yourself, 'I lived through this horror. I can take the next thing that comes along' . . . You must do the thing you think you cannot do."

—ELEANOR ROOSEVELT

❁ Were you lulled into a false sense of security that your labor could be pain-free? If so, spend some time considering this information. Share your perceptions and experience with those you feel offered you unrealistic information.

❁ Every woman experiences pain in an individual way. Your perception of pain is real for you and you have every right to feel your feeling.

❁ Start a "Time Ball" to document all you went through and the fact that you survived more pain than you expected. (You'll find directions for creating a Time Ball in Chapter 5)

❁ Keep talking about the labor pain. Find ways to continue to tell your story.

❀ In some cases, medication cannot be offered after a certain point. Frequently this is to protect the baby.

❀ You deserve to receive both structure and nurture during your labor. Nurture might consist of acknowledging the intensity of the pain; structure might include information about why there are sometimes limitations on the medical staff's ability to reduce pain.

❀ Do not allow this experience to set a pattern for going without care now in your life. This is an isolated experience and should not seep into the rest of your life.

❀ Consider whether someone else's goals were placed on your labor. If you suspect this happened, make efforts to confront the people involved so that you can share how it affected you.

❀ Know that you did not do anything to cause the pain to be so dramatic and neither did your baby.

❀ Practice seeing the pain as good pain, like a powerful wave on the beach, bringing in the tide.

Recognizing Labor Signs

"I was experiencing crampy contractions. I understood that I should stay at home for as long as possible in labor, so I tried to ignore the contractions and get some rest. When I arrived at the hospital, the nursing staff was upset and acted like I should have known. I felt like I had somehow harmed my baby."
—A YAKIMA DISCOVERY GROUP PARTICIPANT

"I knew quite well that someday I must go down this road;
but I had never thought someday would be today."
—NARIHARE, C .870 A.D.

❀ For some women, labor feels like a backache or upset stomach. It does not matter where you did most of your labor. What is critical is that you deliver a baby safely.

❀ All humans do the best we can with the resources we have.

❀ Consider whether you may have received advice prenatally to stay home. If so, visit directly with whoever shared this information with you. Give that person the opportunity to restate the information you heard or to revise the information shared.

Feeling Alone

"Well there I was, all plopped out, legs spread and ready to go. My partner went to get his scrubs on and the medical staff went to get stuff to deliver the baby with. It seemed I was alone. Then I got this amazing sensation—pain that felt like I was coming apart. I screamed and looked between my legs. The doctor was right there. I went into myself. It felt like I was doing this on some remote island and no on was there for me."

—A YAKIMA DISCOVERY GROUP PARTICIPANT

"Come unto me, all ye that labor and are heavy laden,
I will give you rest."
—MATTHEW 11:28

❀ You deserve to receive reassuring words during this time in your labor. It is important to hear reassuring, encouraging and solid messages to help you navigate through the intensity of the urge to push.

❀ Make every attempt to focus on the outcome, meaning the baby was delivered safely.

❀ Validate your experience and make sure to get therapeutic help if this experience has provoked feelings of being unsafe.

❀ Take time to imagine getting the support you wanted. You can even role-play that portion of your labor and stage it the way you prefer.

❀ Remember that you did a fine job of thriving and surviving during labor. Every woman does the best she can—and you are no exception!

❀ Medical professionals thrive in situations in which they can predict the course of their work. When a situation strays from the familiar, a trained doctor may feel caught off guard. When this happens he or she may use words that do not validate the experience a woman is going through. While this is very unfortunate, it does not diminish the quality of care.

Sexual Abuse Memories in Labor

"I had a flashback of being sexually abused during the birth of my baby. Now those memories are whirling in my mind. I am having bad dreams and panicking all the time. I do not want my husband to be around the baby for fear he might be an offender and I do not ever want to leave the baby with anyone."
—A YAKIMA DISCOVERY GROUP PARTICIPANT

*"A new mother must acknowledge this wish for nurturing and
come to terms with it.
In order to protect, she has to feel protected."*
—MARTHA LEQUERICS, PH.D.

❀ You did nothing to make the abuse happen. It was not your fault.

❀ It may take time to feel comfortable expressing yourself sexually. Acknowledge this and get support for yourself and your husband while you recuperate from the birth and from the abuse.

❀ You deserve therapeutic counseling for the trauma you experienced and from the retraumatization you experienced during the birth.

❀ It's normal to feel worried about leaving the baby with anyone. Rather than feeling it is totally your responsibility to protect the child, deal honestly with the problem by getting professional help. Include a family member you trust to be involved in your healing.

❀ Ask for help. In an emergency say, "I need some help from you right now, this is an emergency!" Have a phone list posted for the difficult times when you may be full of feelings and may need some help to think.

❀ It makes sense that you remembered the experience of abuse during birth because of the involvement with your genitals, loss of control, the likelihood that a male was involved and the possibility of pain. Your vulnerable feelings during childbirth may have felt similar, but in reality, the events are very different.

❀ Because of the lack of privacy in your family of origin and the lack of boundaries, it may be helpful to establish additional privacy while you learn to care for yourself and your baby. This is healthy and normal for survivors of sexual abuse.

❀ Humans are amazing creatures. We can block out experiences that are painful. Many do so in order to cope. It is not uncommon for the memories to be stored for many years, with remembrance triggered by life events. Remembering is an ongoing process.

❀ Allow yourself to go at your own individual pace as you learn new methods to build a safe and trustworthy environment.

❀ When feeling any intense emotions, recognize that they are a signal to get support, help, to talk, to learn about the experience. Seek support immediately.

❀ Discovering your sexual abuse can be helpful in subsequent deliveries. It is important for you to share this information with your doctor and with the nursing staff at the hospital. Make a plan for your support people to remind you during labor that you are having a baby and not being abused. Be especially clear about the ways you wish to be touched and to make clear your wishes about pain relief. Some find if helpful to completely block the pain in labor to avoid unhelpful memories.

Noises in Labor

"I am not a loud, boisterous person, but when it came time to finally push in labor, I screamed throughout the entire process, everytime I had a contraction. I later learned that my husband was more alarmed by my screaming than any of the blood he saw. I get a bit embarrassed about how I must have sounded."

—A YAKIMA DISCOVERY GROUP PARTICIPANT

"Noise proves nothing; often a hen who has merely laid an egg cackles as if she had laid an asteroid."

—MARK TWAIN

❀ You survived the most difficult and wondrous event possible for any human being. You are not to be expected to stay in control. You did what was necessary to allow the baby to emerge from the birth canal.

❀ Remember you were in labor! The contractions can be really intense. You have a legitimate reason for crying out.

❀ Nothing is new to the nurses who deliver babies. They have seen it all! Be reassured that they are not taking notes!

❀ Some childbirth experts believe that when a woman is capable of making noises in labor, she is actually more relaxed than if she were to try to "keep it all in."

❀ Talk to those who were with you. Ask their perceptions of the noises you made. It may have been more dramatic for you than for them.

❀ About those preconceived prenatal notions you have about how you thought you would behave—let them go!

A Different Doctor Delivered Your Baby

"I had been told not to go into labor on Wednesday. During the winter that's when my doctor goes skiing. Wouldn't you know it—my water broke on a Wednesday. His recorder said to call the medical exchange to get help from a doctor on call. I could not believe this was happening. The other doctor was supportive, but he didn't know me and hadn't been there during the pregnancy. It impacted how I feel about the entire experience!"

—A Yakima Discovery Group participant

"You can learn more from ten days of agony
than from ten years of content."
—Sally Jesse Raphael

❀ Focus on the skills of adapting you've learned. In pregnancy, as well as in parenting, knowing more than one way to get a job done is important. If you focus too rigidly on only one method to accomplish a goal, you will certainly feel unfulfilled. The survival skills you learned will assist you in life.

Medication Detours

"I had a shot of some narcotic to help me get on top of the contractions. I hated it. I had two of me, one inside crying out for care and one outside that was dopey and not responsive. I could hear people talking to each other about me, but I simply couldn't tell them what I wanted. It was really uncomfortable and I hated it. Next time I'm not going to take that drug."
—A Yakima Discovery Group participant

"Where a doctor cannot do good,
he must be kept from doing harm."
—Hippocrates

❀ Be aware that medications can have an effect on how you perceive the events of your labor. If you have negative memories, take the time to talk with someone to process them.

❀ You deserve accurate and up-to-date information regarding the effects of medication you take. If you did not get appropriate information, let your support team know. Ask them to consider sharing this information with others.

❀ Each person responds differently to medication. Many things go into why a person reacts in a certain way. Those caring for you needed to monitor medication effects. Attempts to communicate with you about how you are feeling needed to be ongoing.

❀ Forgive those members of your support team who may have missed or misinterpreted what was happening. These people did not have experience in the medical world and cannot be expected to translate what was going on.

❀ If you requested help and were not given it, report this information to the supervisors at the hospital. Do not hesitate to complain, whether it was a member of the nursing staff or a physician.

❀ Inquire if there was a medical reason for the events that took place. Sometimes emergencies arise that require the nursing staff to go to another patient who needs care at the same moment.

Cesarean Sections—Unexpected or Expected— and Brief Separations from the Baby

"I was 23 hours on Pitocin, the artificial hormone used to start labor. It was a long, hard labor. The doctors used a vacuum extractor on the baby's head, but we were bone to bone and the baby would not come out vaginally. I had to have a C-section!"

—A YAKIMA DISCOVERY GROUP PARTICIPANT

"I can stand what I know.
It's what I don't know that frightens me."

—FRANCES NEWTON

❀ Most C-sections are performed to save the baby's or mother's life. Few if any C-sections are performed to ease circumstances for the medical staff. Years ago there were problems with unnecessary C-sections. Thanks to advocacy on the part of consumers, there are fewer today.

❀ Any person who goes through a surgery is a survivor of a very stressful experience. You have permission to congratulate yourself for your courage.

❀ Every woman who delivers a baby endures some level of discomfort that complicates memories of the experience.

❀ Reconsider any guilt you feel for not delivering vaginally. The decision to perform a C-section is a medical decision. You are not to blame!

❀ If you were away from your baby just after the birth, be reassured that you can bond with the baby anytime. A short time away from your baby will not affect how you feel about your baby. Calm your fear. Take time to grieve the experience and to express how scared you felt. Talk about any losses you had over not having the labor of your dreams.

❀ Use the "Pop Bead Tool" (in "My Toolshed: Equipment to Enhance My Growth and Development" in Chapter 2) to figure out all the elements of the labor and identify where your attention needs to be focused.

❀ It is no longer expected that once a woman has a C-section she will have to have another. Many women have a vaginal birth after a C-section.

❀ If your C-section was prearranged it was anticipated. It is not uncommon for the event although anticipated, not to turn out as you expected. C-sections are like any birth, full of varied circumstances that keep them from proceeding just the way a person imagined. Avoid blaming yourself and others, rather gather information to resolve any questions you might have.

Asking for What You Need

"I feel I should have known all this stuff but, boy, it sure didn't go like people told me. I kept waiting for people to help me with labor and certainly with breastfeeding. I didn't ask any questions because my friends told me they would tell me what to do. Seems like they didn't tell me a thing and now I'm angry with myself and my friends!"
—A Yakima Discovery Group participant

"God has given us two hands—one to receive with and the other to give with. We are not cisterns made for hoarding. We are channels made for sharing."
—Rev. Billy Graham

❀ Maybe you were cared for in an anticipatory way as a child. This means your caretakers either took care of you by the clock or offered you care when they thought you needed it or when they were available, rather than when you asked for it. People who experience this kind of care as children sometimes never get a chance to develop their own skills for asking for care. If you fit this description, perhaps parenting is your opportunity to relearn ways to ask for care and get your needs met.

❀ The pain of childbirth may have been so dramatic that it has overpowered your ability to get help.

❀ Learn to ask, straight out, rather than manipulate people. Say, "I see you have some ice cream. May I have some too?"

❀ Sometimes a new mother does not hear the infant care instruction offered in the hospital. This may not be because it was not offered, but because there is so much going on that the brain may not take it all in. Also you may have received conflicting information. If you have questions and concerns or need more information, go to a sharing support group, or call the hospital staff or the baby's doctor.

❀ Take your baby's lead. Ask those who are likely to give you what you need. Ask clearly and believe you deserve to get your needs met. You do not have to go without any longer.

❀ Attend a sharing support group to learn from other mothers and learn ways to ask for information.

❀ If you are the oldest, you may be accustomed to helping and giving care. It may be a shift for you to be on the receiving end.

❀ If you are the youngest, your siblings may have cared for you and thought for you. It may be new for you to have to find a way to communicate your needs and make certain you get what you need.

❀ You may be concerned that your ability to receive strokes will decrease now that you have needs, because you are used to getting them instead for all you accomplish.

❀ You have the ability to ask questions, gather information, make and evaluate decisions and to adjust when new information presents itself. Celebrate the experience.

The Memory of Negative Words in Labor

"The words spoken to me by the medical staff were so negative. I felt they were not approving of me. I was in pain and really scared. It hurt my feelings when I overheard them talking in the hall about me. The hurtful words keep running over and over in my mind."

—A YAKIMA DISCOVERY GROUP PARTICIPANT

*"Kind words can be short and easy to speak
but their echoes are truly endless."*

—MOTHER TERESA

❀ Avoid blaming yourself for the feelings of the medical staff. The medical staff may have a built-up resistance to the magnitude of the experience. Because they have seen so many births, they may sometimes forget how vulnerable a new mother feels.

❀ Ask yourself if it's possible that you are remembering these words because they affirm negative beliefs you have about yourself.

❀ Sometimes when people were not cared for well as a child, they "put a face" on someone else. The face is really someone else's—your mother's or father's.

❀ You were a paying customer at the hospital—you deserve an apology. Affirm yourself! Know you deserved nurture and care during this important life transition.

❀ Call up a medical staff person on the phone and share what you heard. Give the person a chance to clarify the words that were said. An explanation may be easy to provide and help to reframe the words.

✽ When confronting the medical person say, "Can we try this again?" or "Can we start over?" Tell her what you needed her to say and exactly how you need her to say it.

Enjoying an Easy Labor

"I was talking to a friend the other day who had a three-day labor that ended in a C-section. When she asked about mine, I said, "I had a three-hour labor." My water broke and I had some small contractions. When we got to the hospital, the nurse examined me and suggested some gentle pushes. The doctor came in, I gave two hard pushes and she was out. I feel sad for my friend, I don't feel like it's fair and I don't want to share my labor at all."

—A YAKIMA DISCOVERY GROUP PARTICIPANT

"Maturity lies in accepting reality,
not in demanding perfection."

—AUTHOR UNKNOWN

✽ You deserve all good things that come your way. Life has its ups and downs, and there's no reason to diminish or discount the ups.

✽ No woman "deserves" easy or difficult labors. For the most part, labors take their own course of action.

✽ If your labor progressed in a different fashion from those described to you, know that the truth is: every labor is different, every woman's response to labor is different.

❀ Keep talking about your labor experience. Remember you could be experiencing a Halo Effect and there may be some pieces you have yet to discover.

❀ Some time in your past you may have received information that suggested that when things go well a person should be quiet. You can revise this belief! Choose to celebrate the wonderful experience you had!

❀ Rarely do people feel that others don't deserve good experiences. If you sense that those around you feel this way, re-evaluate the relationship. Choose to be around people who will celebrate you—and with you.

Postpartum Detours

Unrealistic Expectations

"I remember when I was pregnant, I imagined a Madonna-like life, a glowing mommy and a glowing baby. I guess I forgot that Mary gave birth in a stable with minimal provisions!"
—A YAKIMA DISCOVERY GROUP PARTICIPANT

"Motherhood is not a one-size fits all.
No mother is all good or all bad, all laughing or all serious,
all loving or all angry. Ambivalence runs through their veins.
It is not until you become a mother that your judgment
slowly turns to compassion and understanding."
—ERMA BOMBECK

❀ Evaluate your priorities. Post them in a visible place. When you lean toward perfection of an idyllic dream life, look at what you really believe.

❀ Resolve that you will not get an "A" in every area of your life. Consider that "good enough" is frequently great!

❀ Keep in mind that certain media can cause you to have unrealistic expectations about you, motherhood and life in general. Honor who you are, no matter what.

The Super Mother Syndrome

"I am really feeling disappointed in myself. When I was pregnant I thought nothing would change. I expected that I would be able to keep all the balls in the air. I thought I would get back to normal in no time, that my house would be perfect, the baby would sleep through the night, and we could pick up at a minute's notice and take off. I really was convinced that those who could not keep it all together were weak and that was simply not me! Now that the baby is here I can barely get myself showered and fed, not to mention weeding the garden and polishing the coffee table!

A YAKIMA DISCOVERY GROUP PARTICIPANT

❀ Avoid the lure of attempting to be a super mother. Too often the super mom cares for others and neglects herself.

❀ Consider whether you are willing to sacrifice your health and sanity for the sake of an illusion.

❀ Take one day and one moment at a time. Love yourself. It is healthy to have a vision. Sometimes our wildest dreams are unfilled; sometimes life exceeds our wildest imaginations.

Rest, Eating Well and Exercise vs. Tidiness

"I can't seem to stop the inspiration to keep this house 'picked up.' There's so much extra work with the baby, and because I'm not working for money I feel like I have to keep this place together. I get it all cleaned up and next thing I know it's a mess again! I am exhausted and frustrated!"

—A YAKIMA DISCOVERY GROUP PARTICIPANT

*"With the fearful strain that is on me night and day,
if I did not laugh I should die."*

—ABRAHAM LINCOLN

❃ You have just gone through a physically and emotionally exhausting experience. To complicate matters you are more than likely up all night with your baby. You have good reason to slow down and care for yourself.

❃ Leave your house for part of the day; get away from those four walls telling you to scrub them. Keep one room tidy and let other areas of the house go.

❃ Most children will remember time you spent with them more than a tidy house.

❃ Keep a list of household chores needed to be completed so when someone asks what they can do, you can refer to a list and give them a choice of which household task they are willing to accomplish.

❃ Say to yourself, "I must have sleep to survive." Recognize that sleep is essential to family health and not a postpartum leisure activity.

❀ See the time you spend snuggling with the baby as an investment in the emotional well-being of the child. The house doesn't need an investment in emotional security!

❀ Keep a list of all your accomplishments for the day to reassure you of your need to rest. When you see on paper all you do you will be assured that rest in necessary to keep up the pace.

❀ Remember to eat well and to get a limited amount of exercise, with your physician's approval. Light exercise may give you a feeling of increased energy.

❀ Get out of the house daily for a refreshed perspective.

Work vs. Income

"I had to return to work. My wages pay for our home and our health insurance. I remember the last week at home I held the baby as much as I could and cherished each moment."
—A YAKIMA DISCOVERY GROUP PARTICIPANT

"... the child and her feeling for it were somehow absolute, truer and more bonding than any other experience life had to offer: she felt she lived at the blind true core of life."
—MARILYN FRENCH

❀ Discuss options with your partner. Some might be to work full-time, part-time or flex-time (four 10-hour days with three days off). You could job-share (two or more people share a 40-hour-per-week job).

❀ Create a budget outlining the resources you now have; examine how much the additional income will affect the budget. Consider if it really makes sense for you to return to work.

❀ Think about a trial work period. After a week, a month, or six weeks, evaluate whether to stay or quit. Or, take additional leave without pay. Two or three weeks may be all the extra time you need.

❀ Look for work you can do at home—typing, telemarketing, sewing, starting your own childcare center. You could work evenings or on weekends. Consider working when your partner can care for the baby.

❀ Think about your values and how those values will be transferred to the child if others are caring for the baby.

❀ If you want to stay home and care for your child, seek financial counseling to learn about budgeting and goal setting.

❀ Outline all the housework and get adequate support for sharing those tasks from other adults in the household. Your goal is to avoid working 90-hour weeks and not having enough energy for child-rearing.

Personal Wholeness vs. Codependent Parenthood

"I had a baby to make myself more complete—to have someone love me. Well now she's growing and doesn't need me as much as when she was newborn. Each day I feel like I'm losing her. I hate it when she doesn't want to nurse and prefers to eat solid food. Every time she accomplishes a new feat, it's like one more step to her leaving the nest. People say 'Oh, isn't this great, she's growing up.' I'm supposed to feel that way, but I don't."

—A YAKIMA DISCOVERY GROUP PARTICIPANT

*"If one but realized it, with the onset of the first pangs
of birth pains, it begins to say farewell to the baby.
For no sooner has it entered the world, when others begin
to demand their share. With the child at one's breast,
one keeps the warmth of possession a little longer."*
—Princess Grace of Monaco

❀ The job of parents is to affirm a child's natural growing pace and to encourage that child to do what she/he is naturally propelled to do—grow and become separate.

❀ Parents need to see themselves as whole, complete and separate people. Gain a sense of personal wholeness by experiencing loving care and nurture from others. The beauty of new motherhood is the gift of receiving love rather than relying on the child to fill you up with love.

❀ Think of all the ways, since you've become a parent, you have learned to meet your own needs and found new and interesting ways to connect with support, care and the notion that you are lovable.

❀ Everything we cling to eventually must go. This is a truth of life. Be consciously aware of the feelings of loss you experience as your child grows. Practice honestly asking yourself what your fears are and ask your support team for ways to get your needs met.

Your Self-Worth and the Attention Shift

"My whole pregnancy everyone seemed concerned with how I was feeling. It was hard to go from "main attraction" to "after-thought." My family, friends, and husband were so wrapped up in my baby, I felt left out of the loop! I then felt guilty for being jealous of this perfect little girl. I spoke to my husband and he felt the same way."
—A YAKIMA DISCOVERY GROUP PARTICIPANT

"We are stardust. We are golden
and we've got to get ourselves back to the garden."
—JONI MITCHELL

❀ When you consider that you probably received focused attention for possibly seven or eight months, it is understandable that you miss it.

❀ Considering the seemingly constant onslaught of attention, ranging from numerous baby showers to frequent phone calls regarding the impending delivery, it can be troubling to have the interest shift from you to the infant.

❀ Because it is so difficult to believe a baby is really coming, you may have placed a great deal of focus on your personal experiences, the physical sensations of pregnancy, the hormonal shifts, the changes in relationships and the abundance of concentration on you. It is natural to mourn the shift of attentiveness.

Clothing and Weight

"All the women I know who have new babies seem to be back into pre-pregnancy clothes and managing postpartum better than I am. I thought since my weight gain during the pregnancy had not been excessive that my weight loss after the birth would be easy. Boy, was I ever wrong."

—A YAKIMA DISCOVERY GROUP PARTICIPANT

"The battle to keep up appearances unnecessarily, the mask—
whatever name you give it, creeping perfectionism—
robs us of our energies."

—ROBIN WORTHINGTON

❀ Be patient with your postpartum adjustment. Issues such as weight loss, breastfeeding, schedules or sleep issues, to mention a few, take time to stabilize.

❀ You may look considerably different than you think. You are probably coping significantly better than you are giving yourself credit for.

❀ Avoid dieting. Simply get yourself to eat nutritious, healthy meals, especially if you are breastfeeding.

❀ Call your local hospital or college to get help from a trained dietitian.

❀ Don't expect that breastfeeding will take off the pounds.

❀ Know that every woman is faced with changes in body shape after birth, regardless of how she may appear to the public.

❀ Start a mommy-baby walking group. Contact your hospital to gain sponsorship. This will help to build friends and a healthy habit.

❀ During early postpartum it's good to spend some time alone to get to know the baby, learn how to manage your postpartum body—including breastfeeding—and to get the extra rest you need to survive the round-the-clock feeding of a newborn. Soon though, it will be important for you to get out and connect with other new mothers to share experiences and learn helpful child care tips.

Isolation

"I am scared to take the baby out, I don't fit into any of my clothes and it is a major production to go anywhere. I feel sad and lonely."

—A YAKIMA DISCOVERY GROUP PARTICIPANT

"We're swallowed up only when we are willing for it to happen."

—NATHALIE SARRAUTE

❀ Remember that isolation is the number one enemy of postpartum women. When you are comfortable make every attempt to get together with like-minded people.

❀ Know that in early postpartum it can be helpful to have some time alone to get to know the baby. Very soon though it will be very important for you to get out and connect with other new mothers to share experiences, to learn helpful child care tips.

The amount of time you need to feel comfortable going out in public is up to you. Everyone's different. The circumstances that contribute to the varied degree of willingness to get out are:

❁ The length and intensity of your delivery. You may require more time for rest at home to recuperate.

❁ Whether you have family nearby or whether you may be living in a new area with few outside connections.

❁ Personality type, introvert or extravert. Some people need to be around others the get energy.

❁ Comfort level in public breastfeeding.

❁ Beliefs about when it's safe to take a baby out in public. This varies from culture to culture and community to community based on health and cultural standards.

❁ Simply go outside at least two times a day. Sit on your front porch, go for a walk around the neighborhood, run a short errand to the store. You deserve to have any friends you prefer, to learn from other mothers and to have a community that welcomes you into your new role of motherhood.

Time Away from Your Baby

"I love my baby, but now that she is four months, I want some time away from her. I counted all the hours I have cared for her and they total 2,880. I have never had a job that consumed 24 hours of every day. All my friends seem to manage with this full-time job. I feel so guilty! I can't figure out what to do."
—A YAKIMA DISCOVERY GROUP PARTICIPANT

"Life was meant to be lived."
—ELEANOR ROOSEVELT

❀ Time nurturing yourself during postpartum is food for your soul. You would never consider going without food; neither should you go without nurture.

❀ Remember in elementary school, how you would study, then go outside for recess? Remember how that time away revived you and how you felt ready to get back to work after recess? Imagine how a short recess might fill you up enough to offer the baby better care.

❀ Collect pictures from your favorite home interior magazine; keep them in a colored file folder and browse through them when you need an escape.

❀ Take a five-minute break on your front doorstep and eat a popsicle. See yourself as a more capable, caring parent because you took some time for yourself.

❀ Visualize a five-minute shopping spree. Decide who to go with, choose your peak time of day and pretend to buy something very special.

❀ Visualize a waterfall. Imagine you are in it and that all your anxiety is being washed away, which makes you feel refreshed and energized.

❀ Evaluate the internal voice that may be bombarding you with feelings of guilt. Ask yourself if these are old messages about leisure time from another time in your life and ask yourself if they fit now.

❀ Listen to environmental tapes. You can escape and the baby may be enchanted by the sounds too!

Loss of Control

"I had always planned every element of my life and I had perfect control of my life, now that the baby is here I live in chaos."
—A YAKIMA DISCOVERY GROUP PARTICIPANT

"The feeling of being valuable is a cornerstone of self-discipline, because when you consider yourself valuable, you will take care of yourself."
—M. SCOTT PECK, THE ROAD LESS TRAVELED

"Cleaning your house while your kids are still growing is like shoveling the walk before it stops snowing."
—PHYLLIS DILLER

❋ Visualize a boat in your mind's eye. Put all your worries on the boat and let them go down the stream. If they creep up again, get another boat.

❋ Stop and ask yourself, "Is this issue important? Will it matter in 20 years?" If yes, take care of it; if not, put it on a list for another time.

❋ Say to your friends and family, "If you came to see the house, make an appointment. If you came to see me, come anytime!"

❋ Using calligraphy, make a poster for yourself stating "One thing at a time!"

❋ Say to your partner, "I need some help from you today. Are you able to help me now or later?"

❋ Design a special signal for the outside of your house that telegraphs you are not receiving guests—such as a "Please Don't Disturb!" sign.

Singing the Postpartum Blues

"I have dramatic mood swings,
one minute I am happy the next I am in tears."
—A YAKIMA DISCOVERY GROUP PARTICIPANT

*"Anyone singing the blues is in a deep pit
yelling for help."*
—MAHALIA JACKSON

❀ Get counseling and a physician's consultation anytime in life when you have been diagnosed with any form of depression. The counseling sessions will provide you with a path to help yourself. Do not assume that this challenge will get better all by itself, you need to consult with a professional who can help to diagnose what is happening and help with a plan for your care.

❀ Inquire at your local hospital about a peer-facilitated support group.

❀ Get rest, take babymoons, get outside and ask for help from your support team.

Symptoms of Postpartum Anxiety & Mood Disorders Frequently Called Postpartum Depression

❀ Frequent crying

❀ Wide mood swings

❀ Extended fatigue

❀ Hypochondria

❀ Panic attacks

❀ Confusion, forgetfulness

❀ Feeling distant

❀ Easily angered, or hostile

❀ Depressions, ranging from sadness to suicidal thoughts

❀ Sense of despair and powerless

❀ Nightmares

❀ Weepiness

❀ Hallucinations

❀ Headaches

❀ Numbness

❀ New fears

❀ Extreme guilt

❀ Lack of feeling for the baby

❀ Over-concern for the baby

❀ No energy for anything

❀ Eating disturbances

❀ Feeling out of control

❀ Fear of harming the baby

Finding a Therapist

If you've never sought out professional help, here's how to get started: [1]

❀ Ask friends and family members for a recommendation. Keep in mind that every person is different and that these differences can impact preferences and results.

❀ Meet with the person before you consider a professional arrangement. Ask about training, experience and credentials as well as specialty services. Ask about fees and methods of service.

❀ Make sure when interviewing a therapist that you ask questions, such as: "Have you ever treated individuals with postpartum depression?" "How have your clients reported that they feel better?"

❀ Follow your intuition. Is this someone you believe can guide you in discovering a solution for your concerns?

❀ Therapy will probably generate internal discomfort, which is necessary for growth. If you feel a particular discomfort with your therapist's behavior, find out why. You deserve to feel safe and protected in this relationship. If you're unhappy with it, seek help elsewhere.

Contact your local hospital to see if it will sponsor a confidential postpartum depression support group. Many women have been helped by a "lay-facilitated" support group on this issue.

Changes in Friendships

"My good friend came to visit two weeks after my baby was born. She decided to stay in a hotel so I wouldn't have to 'host' her. When she got here, what she really wanted was to go shopping and lie out by the pool, like the old days. It's 95 degrees out there, blistering hot! No way could I take the baby out! I'm also breast-feeding and not comfortable in public. When I told her 'No,' she was mad. 'I've come all this way! Let's have fun,' she said. Things have changed between us."

—A YAKIMA DISCOVERY GROUP PARTICIPANT

"You can take people as far as they will go, not as far you would like them to go."
—JEANNETTE RANKIN

❁ It is common for friendships to change once a baby is born. This is not about you, your friend or your baby. It's about the circumstances in each person's frame of reference keeping you from undersrtanding each other's experience.

❁ Friends are important in a person's life and when circumstances change the quality of a relationship, it is sad. Grieve the loss.

❁ Write her a letter expressing the current circumstances in your life and how things have changed. Let her know the things you appreciate and the things you wish you didn't have to accommodate. Acknowledge that because she is not experiencing the same thing, it may be challenging to understand but you hope original ties can withstand these changes.

❁ Do not apologize for where you are in your life right now. As a new mother you deserve and need nurture and compassion.

❀ Evaluate the quality of the relationship. Many women find that when they have a baby they are able to see the premise of their friendships more clearly. Sometimes they discover that a friendship is not based on a healthy supportive foundation.

❀ When letting friendships go, honor the time you were friends. Friendships are like flowers planted near each other. One that gets too big for the spot may need transplanting. Transplanting does not diminish the quality of the time spent in that spot.

❀ Attend a postpartum exercise group or start a Baby Brigade, a walking group for parents.

❀ Nurture a friendship with yourself, but avoid becoming isolated and unconnected to the world.

Breastfeeding

"It is unbelievable, my husband goes off to work and I'm sitting on the couch nursing the baby. He comes home at 5:30 and I'm sitting there again, feeding the baby. Me and that couch have gotten to be good friends. I never knew how much a baby ate, sometimes it seems like every hour. What is even harder is that sometimes it takes 45 minutes for the baby to eat, so I spend most of the day sitting and feeding."

—A YAKIMA DISCOVERY GROUP PARTICIPANT

"Who was this immensely powerful person, screaming unintelligibly, sucking my breast until I was in a state of fatigue the likes of which I had never known? Who was he and by what authority had he claimed the right to my life?"
—JEAN LAZARRE

❀ Breastfeeding is very individual. For years some professionals defined successful breastfeeding as a period in which the mother nursed her baby for about a year. The definition of success, however, varies considerably from professional to professional.

❀ A woman's perception about the quality of her mothering is very closely wrapped up in her feeding relationship. The basic goals of feeding, regardless of the method, are to feed the baby and to socialize the baby by a close connection with its mother.

❀ Successful breastfeeding consists of any attempt a woman makes to nurse, regardless of how long and how she feels as a woman as a result of the experience.

❀ Research has shown that one of the significant factors in the length of time a woman breastfeeds and her comfort with breastfeeding is correct knowledge about the baby's latch. What this means is that if your baby is sucking correctly at the breast, your success is increased.

❀ The best way to ensure that your baby is nursing properly at the breast is to have a trained lactation consultant observe a feeding and check the latch. Most hospitals have lactation consultants on staff.

❀ Take time to get to know your baby. New mothers need time alone with their infants to learn the skills of breastfeeding. It can take a few weeks to get the rhythm down, which means you'll need plenty of chances to practice.

❀ Get your breast accustomed to producing adequate amounts of milk by frequently offering the baby a chance to nurse. Your baby must suck at the breast to signal to the breast to make milk. The stimulation by the baby produced by sucking sends a message to your hormonal system to excrete the hormones that tell the breast to make milk.

❀ Get rest! It's essential to make ample milk! Take frequent naps and a babymoon when nursing patterns change. Your emotional state is affected by the amount of rest you have. Your success in managing the hurdles of breastfeeding requires that you be emotionally supported.

❀ You can learn to nurse and rest at the same time by feeding your baby in bed. Let support people take care of the daily routine so you can feed the baby, establish a milk supply and rest.

❀ Scientists have proven beyond a shadow of a doubt that there is a connection between your beliefs about your abilities to feed your baby and your actual ability to do so. Post and use the following affirmations:

- *You deserve nurturing support and helpful information for breastfeeding*
- *Your body is capable of producing enough milk for the baby*
- *Your milk is the perfect food for your baby*
- *You are giving your baby something only you can give*
- *When you breastfeed your baby you are forming a lifelong bond*
- *Your baby will learn to nurse with time and practice*

❀ As your baby grows there will be changes in breastfeeding, growth spurts, learning to manage time away, returning to work, juggling breastfeeding and solid food and eventually weaning. All this requires flexibility. Becoming a mother offers you a chance to master the art of constant change.

❀ During the first year of life, your baby's brain grows to 75% of its eventual adult size! Your child will never go through this level of change again in his life! Your baby will go from a seemingly helpless little person to someone who walks, thinks and talks. During these times of growth the baby may increase time and length of feeding, this is normal.

❀ A vital element in setting goals for breastfeeding is to make them short term. Some women will set weekly goals, others will set daily goals, especially during growth spurts or during initial breastfeeding when nipples can be tender and milk is plentiful.

❀ Breastfeeding mothers are frequently barraged with inaccurate information from family and friends. The most damaging can come from people who have never nursed or who have a bias against breastfeeding. Get connected with people who have accurate, up-to-date information on breastfeeding.

Multiples and Siblings

"I felt violated . . . I became a human incubator for the triplets. Every bit of food was for the babies; every minute of rest was for the babies. The labor room was crowded. Each baby had its own neonatal team. The commotion afterward was overwhelming. Within two minutes the babies were gone to the intensive care unit. There was no bonding time at all."

—A YAKIMA DISCOVERY GROUP PARTICIPANT

"What life means to us is determined not so much by what life brings to us as by the attitude we bring to life; not so much by what happens to us as by our reactions to what happens."

—LEWIS L. DUNNINGTON

❀ Congratulate yourself for surviving this extraordinary event. Throw yourself a survival party.

❀ Link up with other mothers of multiples by mail or phone. Or start your own Discovery Group.

❀ Adopt the "Crunch a Bunch of Family Love" concept where you begin to see that the quality of interactions between people can be enhanced when there are more people. Your children will be crunching more love into each minute because there are more people to give love!

❀ Count all the chances for increased support for your children. Studies show that the more people a child has on her or his support team, the more likely she or he will be to succeed into adulthood in a healthy fashion.

❀ Make a quilt representing all the members of your family. Each block of the quilt can represent a member of your family and be a visual reminder of all the additional love available to each person.

❀ Start a charm bracelet with inexpensive charms that symbolize the members of your family.

❀ Build a garden spot for each child and connect them with an herb hedge formed in an infinity sign. The infinity sign is a symbol in mathematics of something that lasts forever and continues for all time.

❀ Frame a picture of you and *your* siblings. Ask yourself if you need to grieve the birth of one of your siblings, which reduced the amount of care and attention you received as a child.

❀ Design a totem pole, using wood, clay, or paper to represent all the members of your family. Put the people on the totem pole in the order of their births. Don't forget to put yourself at the top.

Death of a Relative

"My grandmother died 20 days before my baby was born. The hardest part was knowing I missed out on seeing the two of them meet. My mother told me, 'When a baby smiles, the angels are whispering to her.' My husband changed it to 'When a baby smiles, grandmas are whispering to her.' I miss her."

—A Yakima Discovery Group participant

"The farther one travels on the journey of life, the more births one will experience, and therefore the more deaths—the more joy and the more pain. But for all that is given up, even more is gained."

—M. Scott Peck,
The Road Less Traveled

❀ Create a memory book of all the memorabilia that you collected during the time of your family member's passing.

❀ Plant flowers, such as a rose bush or a flowering bush that would bloom near the birthday of the one you lost. This will commemorate the death of your family member and the birth of your child.

❀ Place Post it™ notes around the house with your favorite statement frequently uttered by the person who has died.

❀ Keep a running journal of all of the things you wished you had said to the person who died.

❀ Draw a picture of your feelings. This will help you to get in tune with your childlike feelings.

❀ Decorate the grave on important days and anniversaries and include your child in the ceremony.

Baby Detours

The Way Your Baby Looks—
Unkind Labels

"I had dreamt about what my child would look like for many years. When the baby was born, covered with blood, puffy eyes and kind of wrinkled, I was really upset. He didn't look like the Gerber baby one bit."
—A YAKIMA DISCOVERY GROUP PARTICIPANT

"All God's children are not beautiful.
Most of God's children are, in fact, barely presentable."
—FRAN LIEBOWITZ

The compression of the contractions and the nature of the cramped birth canal can take its toll on the appearance of the newborn. Some babies have rather misshapen heads caused by the normal molding to the shape of the birth canal. Some even appear to have a cone-shaped head.

Many babies emerge from the womb covered in vernix. This "cheese like" covering is the substance that protected the baby's skin from long exposure to amniotic fluid. While seemingly unsightly, it is high in emolient factors and good for the skin of the baby.

Due to the exchange of hormones from mother to baby, infants occasionally will have swollen breasts and genitals. These phenomena will decrease as the baby's system metabolizes and breaks down the hormones from its mother.

In order that they stay warm in-utero, most babies are covered with lanugo, a fine cottony hair covering the head, shoulders, back, forehead and temples.

Occasionally some babies will have puffy eyes after they are born. The tremendous pushing of the baby through the birth canal is one cause of puffy eyes. Another cause can be antibiotic ointment that is placed in the eyes shortly after birth to protect them from venereal diseases.

The reddened areas on the eyelids or back of the neck of newborns are called "stork bites," which are due to the thin layer of developing skin in these areas. Most will fade in the months to come; some may take a year.

Some Caucasian babies may have "angel kisses," a reddened area between their eyes. These spots are also considered normal and thought to be caused by the thinness of the layer of skin in that area.

"Mongolian Spot," a bruise-like colored spot on the bottom of Asian, Southern European and Black babies is also normal. This spot fades with age and typically disappears soon after age two.

Many newborns are plagued with rashes, frequently looking like a profuse outbreak of tiny white-headed pimples. These rashes are temporary and typically disappear at around four weeks, with no special treatment required. These normal newborn rashes are caused by the baby's skin adjusting to life outside of the womb.

❀ These minor appearance irritants are temporary and will change as the baby acclimates to his/her new world.

❀ Ignore unkind words spoken about your baby. Do not give those who make these statements any attention. Talk to the baby about what you really see. Say, "Do not misunderstand them. They do not have accurate information. You are a healthy child, growing at a pace that's right for you."

❀ Evaluate negative labels you may have heard as a child. Throw them out.

Learning Your Baby's Language

"When I was expecting a baby I had no clue what colic is. No way was I prepared for the hours of uncontrollable screaming. From the moment he wakes up to the minute he goes to sleep, he cries. People keep telling me to relax, as if I was making him cry. It hurt my feelings. I expected we would connect and I would enjoy the baby, but those moments are few."

—A YAKIMA DISCOVERY GROUP PARTICIPANT

"Who is getting the pleasure from this rocking,
the baby or me?"
—NANCY THAYER

❀ Human beings are not instinctual parents. Learning to care for a baby takes time and patience. The amount of crying a baby does is never a definition of a good baby or a bad baby. Infant crying is a form of communication.

❀ Congratulate your baby for calling out for the care she needs. Say, "I see you need something. I am going to do my best to help you."

❀ When you are frustrated and cannot figure out what the baby needs, you can say, "I have done everything I know how to do. I know this is uncomfortable for you. Know that I love you and will keep trying to learn about you so that I can meet your needs."

❀ Remember that you are doing the best you can with the resources you have. You are a bright and intelligent person who can learn new ideas and use them.

❀ Babies have personality temperaments, too. Some are introverts and some are extraverts. Spend time determining which personality your baby seems to have and honor it, offering your baby opportunities to get his needs met in the style that fits him best.

❀ Your baby is not trying to control you; the baby's cries are designed to ensure survival. If he could talk to you, he would tell you exactly what he needs. A crying infant may simply be saying, "I want to be with you."

❀ Learn your baby's language. Learn which signals mean that she wants some care. Babies will signal in subtle ways. For some, crying is a last resort when the other ways of saying "care for me" do not get their caregiver's attention. Pediatrician and researcher T. Berry Brazelton, M.D. says infants communicate in a variety of ways:

A baby who wants your attention communicates by:
- Smiling.
- Looking directly at you.
- Making ballet-like peaceful movements.
- Looking toward the person chosen to give her care.
- Trying to talk to you or by making mouth movements.

- Opening her eyes, curiously bright, very wide.
- Producing a shiny and bright face.
- Perching and stretching toward you.

An infant who wants to be left alone or wants you to stop whatever you are doing communicates by:
- Turning his face away from you.
- Relaxing, which changes his skin color to a pale or reddish tint.
- Becoming fussy.
- Producing hiccoughs.
- Spitting up his food.
- Falling asleep.
- Kicking or squirming.
- Increasing the pace of his breathing.
- Yawning.
- Wrinkling his forehead or frowning.

❀ Get frequent and predictable times away from your baby. People, including mothers, deserve a break from their activities of the day.

Remember: A crying baby does not mean you are an incompetent parent. Nor does it mean that your baby does not love you. It simply means that the baby is attempting to communicate.

Your Baby's Sleep Patterns

"I have never been so tired in all my life! This baby does not sleep during the day or at night. No one told me I would be up and down all night long. I have been doing this now for 5-1/2 weeks with no rest in sight. I feel like a terrible mother. People say, 'Is he a good baby? Does he sleep at night?'"

—A YAKIMA DISCOVERY GROUP PARTICIPANT

*"If a child is to keep alive his inborn sense of wonder,
he needs the companionship of at least one adult who can
share it, rediscovering with him the joy, excitement and
mystery of the world we live in."*
—RACHEL CARSON

❀ Researchers have determined that five hours straight is equivalent to "sleeping through the night" for a baby under age one. It is believed that babies alternately sleep through the night, then waken later due to all the growing they do in their first year of life.

❀ Babies are neither good nor bad because of sleep patterns. Imagine someone asking, "Is your husband good? Does he sleep through the night?"

❀ There is no correlation between breastfeeding quality and the amount of sleep a baby gets.

❀ You cannot spoil a baby by answering his calls at night. Practice seeing your parenting as having nothing to do with a clock.

❀ Research in the brain activity of babies proves that their sleep cycle is different from that of adults.

❀ Babies practice new skills, like rolling over, pulling up on things, crawling at night as well as during the day. Sleep may be interrupted by teething, ear infections, and changes in schedules.

❀ Infant sleep is related to survival issues, not control issues. Babies are wired to wake at night to ensure they have enough food to support their growth.

❀ Remember to rest when the baby rests.

Your Adopted Baby

"I had always wanted to have a baby. All my life I planned to be a mother. I was heartbroken when we were unable to produce a child. After years of fertility procedures, we decided to adopt. We waited years for a baby. Then, suddenly all we had was two days' notice. It was overwhelming. As it turned out, though, we were able to be present at the birth of our daughter. The whole experience was bittersweet—joyful and sad!"

—A Yakima Discovery Group participant

"So for the mother's sake the child was dear,
And dearer was the mother for the child."
—Samuel Taylor Coleridge

❀ Give yourself time to adjust. Regardless how long you have wanted a baby, it can still be a shock to the system.

❀ You will go through all the normal grieving processes of a woman who has delivered a child. While you may not have to physically recover from labor, you may have to emotionally adjust to managing a baby.

❀ Expect times of rough adjustment, no matter how thrilled you are.

❀ Connect with other mothers, whether they are women who adopted or not. Anyone caring for a baby and building a family needs support.

❀ Practice loving yourself and your body. Rid yourself of any hurt, shame or guilt you have felt about not being able to become pregnant.

❀ Focus on today and see yourself as deserving the joys that come your way. You deserve to feel whole—not because of what you are able to do, but just because of who you are!

❀ Focus on the skills in resiliency you develop from the adoption experience. Practice honoring how they will help in life and as a parent.

The Child You Lost

"I gave a baby up for adoption. Now that my new baby is here, I keep thinking about my first-born. People ask me if this is my first and I'm at a loss for what to say. Sometimes I wonder where she is and how she's doing. From time to time, my mind drifts back to 10 years ago. I remember the smells, the words and the pain. I so much love my new baby, but, sometimes I wonder if I'm able to be a good mother, if I am a good person."

—A YAKIMA DISCOVERY GROUP PARTICIPANT

"If snow falls on the far field where travelers spend the night, I ask you, crane, to warm my child in your wings."

—ANONYMOUS

❀ Create rituals to celebrate the birthday and any other important days around the birth of your first child.

❀ Practice seeing yourself as allowing someone else to parent your child, rather than seeing yourself as someone who gave up or abandoned the child. Honor that you are a mother of two children—one who is being parented by others and one whom you are parenting.

❀ Practice saying to yourself, "You did the most wonderful thing any person can do for another—you gave your body to allow another person to grow and have a life."

❀ Avoid comparing the new baby to the one you relinquished. No one deserves to be compared, especially when the person being compared is not present.

❀ Seek out support for the parenting you are doing right now. Start a sharing support group for new mothers.

❀ Practice cherishing the moments you shared with your first baby during pregnancy. In truth, pregnancy is the only time we are really and truly connected with our babies.

❀ Go gently with yourself as you share your life experiences. Find caring, loving people who will not judge you. Remember that you are lovable for who you are, not for the things you did or did not do.

❀ Take time to reframe any negative experiences associated with the first birth, and review pertinent detours in this book to help you process.

CHAPTER 10

Building a Sharing Support Group

*"We may have all come on different ships,
but we're in the same boat now."*
—Martin Luther King

I f you think you would do your best exploration in a group but
there is no group nearby, you may want to consider starting
your own community Discovery Group.™

Why Start a Discovery Group?

The purpose of a Discovery Group is to support your journey
of becoming a mother. Such a group can help you resolve,
reframe or rework expectations and beliefs. It can also support the
steps you take to seek a safe passage for you and your baby during
the childbearing journey.

The childbearing year is a major life experience for you as a
woman. The Discovery Group can help you accept the magnitude of

this responsibility and help you care for your baby by sharing and learning information from other women parenting similar-aged children.

Providing you with a constant and consistent opportunity to interact with other new mothers, a Discovery Group can decrease the negative effects you may be feeling as a result of being isolated at home with a small child or several small children.

In addition to allowing you to tap in to the wisdom you have gained in becoming a mother and providing a way to share your wisdom with others, such a group will help mother *you*, the just-born mother, by constantly encouraging you to accept nurture from the group and by highlighting the opportunities to recycle your own developmental needs.

Meeting Format for a
Parent-Infant Sharing Support Group

I. Introduction

❀ Begin the meeting on time.

❀ Let participants know where to find the rest room and available beverages. Encourage them to use the rest room, care for themselves and their babies as they see fit.

❀ Read aloud the posted "Ground Rules," they are:[1]

  • Everyone participates
  • Right to pass
  • All beliefs are honored
  • Mutual respect
  • Confidentiality

❀ Read aloud the "Discovery Group Beliefs and Themes" poster to explain the purpose of the group. Go over these at each meeting to set up an atmosphere of support and nurture. Examples of such themes are:[2]

  • Children are important.
  • Adults are important.
  • Children deserve helpful interactions with adults.
  • Adults deserve to break the chains of uneven parenting they received.
  • People can celebrate their strengths.

II. Introduction of Mothers

Ask each mother to do the following:

❀ Introduce herself and her baby.

❀ Tell when the baby was born and how old the baby is.

❀ Facilitator should choose one of the following additional, optional questions and have each woman respond:

- Tell us something you are wondering.

- Tell us something you cannot believe you would ever be doing that you *are* doing because you had this baby.

- Tell us something someone said that was very helpful.

- Tell us something said about having a baby that was outrageously untrue.

- Tell us something you thought for sure would happen that did not.

- Tell us the funniest thing that has happened since the birth of the baby.

- Tell us one thing you wish had happened that did not.

III. Sharing Successes

❀ Following introductions, begin the sharing by going around the circle and asking each person to share a success or celebration with the group. Invite each woman to share a success on the "mommy scale"—where small things count as measurable successes. Things like getting the dishes done or a baby who sleeps through the night are very meaningful to a new mom.

❀ Use humor whenever appropriate.

❀ Stress that accomplishments will be different now for the new mother. She may not be able to accomplish as much or the same after the birth of her baby. Note that she has not lost her abilities, but that different, less measurable projects are now making good use of those abilities.

❀ Encourage new mothers to see the successes, no matter how seemingly small, in the real world and count them! It is very hard to measure all the effort and work that goes into caring for a baby!

❀ The facilitator or leader can list accomplishments by writing them on butcher paper or any chart or blackboard so that every mother can see all that the group has to celebrate.

❀ Always allow members of the group the "right to pass" and remember to thank all who contribute, including those who pass.

❀ Once each month, offer time for the women to share their birth stories. They sincerely enjoy this, regardless of how many times they have told their stories. Aside from being informative to those who are new to the group, the women experience increased depth of understanding each time they share this momentous occasion in the history of their lives.

IV. Sharing Concerns, Problems and Challenges

After each person has had a chance to share her success, go around the room again and ask each person if she came to group with a specific *concern, problem or challenge* for which she needs support.

Because each person is different and because new mothers perceive that they have few choices, I recommend offering a number of ways to solve problems. A few of the exercises we use are provided in the Toolshed at the end of this chapter.

Offer those who have a concern a choice of one of the following:

❈ Asking for Factual Information
❈ The Suggestion Circle
❈ The Tally Sheet
❈ The Safety Plan

V. Closing

❈ Approximately five minutes before closing, have participants state any resentments and appreciations regarding the activities of the day.

❈ Close by saying, "Practice seeing yourself as the lovable, capable person that you are. Remember that you are in charge of your self-esteem and can find ways of getting and giving strokes every day."

Criteria of a Successful Discovery Group

One of the most important elements for running a successful Discovery Group is finding a comfortable room with close, easy access to parking. If the location is confusing to reach, use clearly marked signs that mothers can easily follow.

Begin the Discovery Group on time but reassure mothers that coming late is okay. Always post "Ground Rules" and go over them each meeting to set up an atmosphere of support and nurture.

❀ **Weekly meetings.** Offer the Parent-Baby Sharing Group weekly.

❀ **Come when you can.** Stress that the design of the group is on a "come when you can" basis. This assures participants that they don't have to make a commitment to the group. They are welcome to join whenever things slow down or when they feel a need for support.

❀ **Late morning.** Schedule the group late in the morning. Many new moms have been up all night and don't take kindly to an early morning schedule.

❀ **Comfort.** Stress that they should come as they are. The Discovery Group is the one place where everyone will understand if you show up with wet hair!

❀ **Proximity.** New mothers in the group tend to sit next to the facilitator. You might save a spot for new members to sit on each side of you so they feel protected. For many women, early postpartum is accompanied by strong feelings and they prefer not to be put on the spot. It is best to start the discussion with members who have been in the group before.

❀ **Format.** Avoid changing the format too frequently. Women may benefit by experiencing a predictable format considering that their lives with their babies are now very unpredictable. The format design can be evaluated by the group on a quarterly basis.

❀ **Childcare.** Provide childcare for older siblings. Many women are mourning the loss of the intimacy they had with their older child. Based on the predictable struggles many of the siblings go through as they adjust, we find it important to provide a place where mothers can express their feelings with their older child out of earshot.

❀ **Music.** Use a tape recorder to play soft music as mothers come in. Also, choose a theme song to play at each meeting before you start the group discussion to signal that the program is about to begin.

❀ **Developmental affirmation posters.** Like those shown on page 145. You can order the ones we use from Jean Illsley Clarke, Daisy Press, 6535 Ninth Avenue, North Plymouth, MN 55447. Perhaps you'll want to create your own with permission.

❀ **Handouts.** Provide them on infant care and postpartum issues that you discover in magazines, newsletters or hospital information. Or you can order special handouts from ICEA, called The Better Baby Series, P. O. Box 20048, Minneapolis, MN 55420; (617) 854-8660. For a catalog or special orders, call (800) 624-4934.

❀ **Postpartum depression symptoms.** Put up a poster at every meeting so mothers can monitor their adjustment to this phase of their lives. (See Postpartum Detours in Chapter 9.)

❀ **Name tags.** Write both the mother's and baby's names on name tags so that women can get to know each other.

❀ **Sign-in sheet.** Lay out a sign-in sheet with "You Have Every Right to Be Here" printed at the top. This may appeal more to mothers who are visual learners and believe positive strokes more when they are written. Ask new mothers to write in their addresses and telephone numbers.

❀ **Do not disturb.** Post a "Please Don't Disturb" sign on the outside door to help everyone feel more comfortable. Many women learning to breastfeed will appreciate not having to worry about unexpected visitors.

❀ **Beverages.** Provide beverages, especially lots of ice water, decaf, tea, or juice for thirsty, nursing mothers.

❀ **Library.** Encourage a "Discovery Group Library." Mothers can lend books from their personal libraries to each other. This enables mothers to share valuable information on caring for their children or any other topic.

❀ **Tissues.** Keep plenty of tissues around for postpartum women experiencing highs and lows.

Sensitive Topics and Confidentiality

Confidentiality is critical to the health and well-being of group participants. When reading the Ground Rules, ask each person to promise to keep the specifics of the meeting quiet.

❀ Have available a list of local counseling services that includes those organizations accepting medical coupons or that provide services on a sliding scale. Provide a handout on how to find a therapist.

❀ If possible, provide a skill-based childcare class for interested participants. Parent education topics can be integrated into the discussion by the facilitator, but the format is not designed to teach infant feeding, for example.

❀ An affiliation with the medical community is helpful for the success of the mother/baby support group. Health care providers benefit greatly when there is a system in place to support new mothers' adaptations to parenting. Childcare concerns may need to be referred to the medical community. If possible, partner this service with the local maternity unit or a local physician.

Outline for a Discovery Group Facilitator

Materials You'll Need:

- Tape recorder and tapes
- Name tags
- Suggestion Circle poster
- Affirmation posters
- Safety Plan sheet
- Plenty of tissues

- Sign-in sheet
- Ground Rules poster
- Postpartum Depression poster
- Suggestion Circle sheets
- Discovery Group Tally sheet

Tools You'll Use:

- Asking for Factual Information
- Suggestion Circle

- The Discovery Group Tally
- The Safety Plan

Meeting Format Overview

I. Opening
Introduce yourself.
Explain the function of the group.

II. Safety and Ground Rules
Place a "Please Do Not Disturb" sign on the outside of door.
Review the ground rules.

III. Beliefs and Themes
Review the "Beliefs and Themes" poster.

IV. Introductions
Ask each member to introduce herself and her child.
Ask each member a question that gets her focused on the group.

V. Discussions
Birth Stories. Offer a time to share birth stories once a month.
Share Celebrations.
Share Concerns, Problems or Challenges.

VI. Upcoming Events
Announce any events to come for children and families.

VII. Closing Statement

MY TOOLSHED:
DISCOVERY GROUP

I. Asking for Factual Information

❀ The mother asks a question.

❀ Participants are allowed to provide information that can be found in writing or information for which the source was an expert on the issue, such as a physician or a nutritionist.

❀ Three responses are taken from the group.

❀ The information is written down for the asking mother.

MY TOOLSHED:
DISCOVERY GROUP

II. Suggestion Circle[3]

Purpose

❁ To help new mothers who seek information about alternative solutions to specific problems.

❁ To assist new mothers in activating clear thinking as well as tapping into the wisdom of the group.

❁ To help new mothers who feel they can acquire valuable skills for parenting.

The Suggestion Circle may be used by individuals as well as groups. New mothers can learn to use it and call support people on the phone or write them requesting their best suggestion on specific concerns in your life.

Rules for Suggestion Circle

❁ *Say:*

"Now it's time to think about our concerns, problems or challenges. I invite you to think of a problem, a challenge or concern that you might have and would like suggestions for. The problem you share can be about any issue in your family life." Using all three words—concern, problem and challenge—gets the women to take part in the process.

❀ Post the Suggestion Circle rule poster.

❀ Review the rules and hold up the poster as you do.

❀ Mother with problem states clearly in one sentence the problem she needs suggestions for.

❀ The mother with the problem then becomes the listener.

❀ Ask two people to record on a piece of paper all the suggestions for the mother to take home. One person writes one suggestion and the other writes the next.

❀ Offer the group a chance to ask clarifying questions so that they can give the best possible suggestions for the situation. Take three questions from the group.

❀ Then, go around the circle, providing each participant the opportunity to offer her suggestion.

❀ Ask the people in the group to think carefully for a moment and formulate their best possible suggestions. The goal is to gather a list of high-quality, concise alternatives.

❀ Remind the listener to say, "Thank you," after each suggestion—even to those who pass.

❀ Remind the listener to *not* evaluate the suggestions right there on the spot. Concerned for her, we are also concerned about the self-esteem of the women providing the suggestions. It also keeps the listener from saying, "Yeah, but . . ." and discounting the quality of the suggestions.

❀ The women offering suggestions are asked to not personalize the suggestions. If someone begins to say, "This happened to me too, and I did . . . ," say to that person, "Remember, tell her what to do . . ." or "Remember the rules . . ." They can use such statements as:

- "Read this book . . ."
- "Buy this product . . ."
- "Say this statement . . ."
- "Think about . . ."
- "Remember that . . ."
- "Know that . . ."

❀ Encourage the women to make their suggestions as quickly as possible. The goal is to gather as much information as quickly as possible so that the group can address everyone's issue.

❀ If a woman does not have a suggestion, or is not sure that her suggestion will be helpful, or if someone else mentioned her suggestion before it was her turn, have her say, "I pass."

❀ When all the suggestions have been given, ask the listener if she wishes to hear second suggestions. If the answer is yes, go around the circle again.

❀ The leader can offer suggestions too, but it is helpful to pass sometimes to avoid always appearing the expert.

❀ When all the suggestions have been gathered say, "Now (insert the listener's name) we invite you to think, choose and use the suggestions that work best for your family."

❀ Have the people who were recording the suggestions pass the sheets with the suggestions to the listener. Wish her well!

MY TOOLSHED:
DISCOVERY GROUP

III. Discovery Group Tally Sheet

Purpose

The GOAL OF THE DISCOVERY GROUP TALLY SHEET is to gather data from the support group for a mother who is concerned about a problem and wants to know: (1) if others have gone through the problem, (2) when the problem occurred, (3) how many women experienced the concern and (4) how it was resolved.

This gathering of averages keeps conversation manipulators from taking over. This tool also offers a mother unbiased data she can use to validate her guesses. She can then ask for a Suggestion Circle or wait until the problem works itself out via natural development of the child.

Further, the Tally Sheet keeps the facilitator from answering from her collective personal or professional experience.

Example: A mother whose baby was five weeks old asked when other mothers in the group felt they were into a rhythm or a somewhat predictable napping and night-time sleeping schedule. She also wondered whether the mothers led the child to the sleep schedule or the baby naturally fell into a regular routine. Finally, she wanted to know at what age all this happened.

❀ The facilitator asked the group to consider the following questions:

1. Did the mother lead or did the baby lead?
2. What was sleep routine during the day?
3. What was sleep routine during the night?
4. At what age did it happen?

❀ That day the facilitator counted 13 mothers and 13 babies present. She drew a quick Tally Sheet that looked like the following:

Daytime Sleep Routine (Questions 1 and 2)

Mother Lead	Both	Baby Lead
1	1	11

Nighttime Sleep Routine (Questions 1 and 3)

Mother Lead	Both	Baby Lead
3	2	8

The Baby's Age When It Happened (Question 4)

Age	Number of Babies Establishing Routine
2 weeks	1
6 weeks	2
7-1/2 weeks	1
2 months	1
9 weeks	2
2-1/2 months	1
12 weeks	4
cannot remember	1

What we were able to determine for this mother is that the average age for a baby to mold into a routine was somewhere between nine and twelve weeks. Of the mothers who were present that day, a majority allowed the baby to mature into routine for both day and night sleep patterns.

This informal data gathering instilled faith in this mother that she and her baby were on the right track, and that there would be a light at the end of the tunnel within the next four to six weeks. She then asked for a Suggestion Circle to survive the next six weeks.

The Tally Sheet is a way to gather information that helps mothers come to their own conclusions about:

❀ Whether an issue is a problem, and
❀ Whether they should do something about it.

Steps to Facilitate the Tally

❀ Listen to the problem. It will begin with: "I would like to know how many of you . . .?" or "When did your baby do . . .?"

❀ Determine the various parts to be tallied. Write them on a sheet of paper.

❀ Ask each mother to report the information she remembers that relates to the question. Write each response in the appropriate place on the sheet.

❀ Mathematically determine the averages that come up and report the figures to the group.

❀ Give the Tally Sheet to the mother to use as a reminder or to share with family members.

Caution: Do not use this sheet if you know or suspect that the woman is the only person in the room with this problem. It may cause her to feel even more isolated. This technique works best when gathering information on normal growth and development issues. Some relationship issues can be also tallied but please use discretion!

IV. The Safety Plan

Purpose

THE FIRST AND MOST IMPORTANT NOTION in terms of personal safety is to know that all human beings deserve to be in nurturing, supportive relationships. All people were put on earth to be loved and cared for.

The Goal of the Safety Plan

The Safety Plan is designed to assist a new mother when:

1. Her personal safety is at risk.
   Example: Someone is physically, emotionally or sexually abusing her.
2. The personal safety of a mother/group member's children is at risk.
   Example: Someone is physically, emotionally or sexually abusing her child.

Rules

This plan is designed to help her think clearly during times of great emotional distress and to:

- ❀ Clarify her beliefs or position on the issue.
- ❀ Determine and name her helper(s) during the event. It is important if her personal safety is at risk for the group/the facilitator to have on hand an accessible list of resources for help. It is recommended that you list the names of a number of resources.

❀ Decide what role her support team will play to ensure safety. Write down exactly what they agreed to do.

❀ Determine what could get in the way of the team assisting in the way they agreed. By determining what obstacle her support team might have in assisting her with her safety, she will be able to analyze the need for additional backup systems.

❀ Determine what is likely to be the hardest part about achieving personal safety. Acknowledge the hardest part about taking the next step. For each person this will be different. Usually this has to do with emotional ideas we have about our abilities. Frequently these ideas have been placed in our minds by our abusers, to keep us enslaved in the abuse cycle.

❀ List any signs that the safety plan is going badly.

❀ After achieving the safety needed, make a list to share with your support group. Include the additional support you will need.

There are many other activities that can be used in a Discovery Group. Perhaps you'll come up with some of your own. If you'd like more information based on our experience using these groups, I hope you'll let me know. I'd also like to know how you are progressing on your childbearing journey. Feel free to write me and let me know how this material was helpful for you as a mother.

If you wish to obtain information on professional training in Discovery Group development or training in the use, with parents, of other materials featured in the *Journey of Becoming a Mother*, please contact me in care of the Love and Logic Press, Inc.

Laurie Kanyer
THE LOVE AND LOGIC PRESS, INC.
2207 Jackson Street
Golden, Colorado 80401

Dear Reader,

Congratulations, on completing *The Journey of Becoming a Mother: Tools for a New Mother's Emotional Growth and Development*. Find ways to absorb the accomplishment you have just made in growing through this book. Honor the fact that, during one of the greatest times of change known to humankind, you found ways to support your emotional growth and development. This is no small task for a woman to accomplish during any time in her life, not to mention during new parenthood! You are truly amazing!

The Journey of Becoming a Mother offered you abundant materials designed to enhance your childbearing journey. Remember you are a bright, capable person, able to think and make decisions that fit your unique situation. Please continue to think, select and use only that information that works best for you. You can hold tightly to what you believe and allow new ideas to soak into the garden bed of your life at a pace most helpful to you.

Ellen Rhoades, a mother in the Yakima Discovery Group reminds us that, "A flower about ready to bloom is as beautiful as a freshly cut flower." The flower that is you knows how to get what you need, in your distinctive and exceptional way. You are invited to choose to use the ideas that will nourish the variety of flower you are becoming and the family you are growing.

Cherish what bloomed in your childbearing year, find ways to get to know those things that came to be, which you could not have anticipated and know you can find ways to take the steps you need to take toward emotional health and well-being. Know the decision is yours and the invitation is always here!

"You are the caretaker of the generation,
you are the birth giver," the sun told the woman.
"You will be the carrier of this universe."
—BRULE SIOUX SUN CREATION MYTH

Laurie A. Kanyer
Certified Family Life Educator

TERMS USED IN THE BOOK

Adapted or Racquet Feelings- Feelings that humans choose to feel because the feelings are acceptable in the group they live in. Humans adapt to feelings that may not be most helpful in a particular situation, but are feelings sanctioned in the group they live in. In many cases the price of feeling the most appropriate feeling is very high, so they adapt to use the sanctioned adapted or racquet feelings to remain safe in the family group they live in.

Affirmation- A powerful, positive message—verbal or nonverbal—that can help to define a person's self-esteem. They can be given to us by other people and by ourselves.[1]

Archaic Beliefs- Archaic beliefs are beliefs from the past about a person's feelings of self-worth that no longer fit today. Frequently archaic beliefs do not match reality and are projected onto someone by another person. The opportunity presented in the childbearing journey is one of looking objectively at all the data regarding who we are and examining whether it is valid.

The Childbearing Year- The childbearing year can last from the time a woman considers becoming pregnant until that baby starts to sleep through the night or weans from the bottle or breast (typically around one year of age) The five components are "Pre-pregnancy," "Pregnancy," "Birth," "Early Postpartum," and "Settling In-Deciding to Be."

Conclusions of Self- Beliefs that a person has adopted about their self-worth based on the quality of support offered to the person. Conclusions from the core of our self-esteem. They can be revised and changed at anytime.

Decisions- Ideas about a person's self-esteem and life path can be made based on the quality of data offered to them about who they are and about their individual worth. Also these "decisions" are beliefs a person has formed about how they must behave in order to get strokes.

Detours- "Detours," are experiences that get in the way of healthy development for a woman during her childbearing year. A detour is a glitch that can impact a woman's emotional self during the childbearing journey. Frequently not overly dramatic, but detours tend to affect the way women view the childbearing experience and for some women they may effect self-esteem. Childbearing experiences tend to stick with a woman, planting firmly in their memory. Unpleasant "detours" can create troublesome spots in family life.

Developmental Stage- Human beings develop in a systematic progression that is predictable. Like the scenes in a play, for each age of a human being's life they have an opportunity to gain certain predictable skills. Each age a person goes through is called a developmental stage. Jean Illsley Clarke and Connie Dawson, authors of *Growing Up Again* share, "We all go through stages as we grow and each stage is important. A developmental stage is a describable segment of growing up. During each stage the person is busy with age-appropriate tasks that help answer the all-important questions: Who am I? And who am I in relation to others? How do I acquire skills that I need?"[2]

Developmental Task- In each developmental stage there is a series of jobs, skills or tasks that are predictable and expected to be accomplished. Developmental tasks are the expected series of growth skills that can be anticipated for each phase of human development.

Environment- An environment is the place one resides. For use in this book an environment includes the planned support that a woman asks for and receives during childbearing. The contents of each person's environment may be different, based on their individual preferences.

Extravert- Mary Sheedy Kurcinka author of *Raising Your Spirited Child* defines extraverts as, "People who draw their energy from others. They prefer to engage the world around them outside of their bodies by talking with people, sharing ideas and experiences."[3]

Frame of Reference- A frame of reference is a collection of varied experiences and beliefs that contribute to the way people look at the world. It is the multitude of beliefs, values and processes, including our cultural and spiritual backgrounds, that contribute to the way we function in the world. We hold our frame of reference very dearly because it describes the collection of experiences validating our own personal corner of the world. The information on a frame of reference can be changed and adapted to fit new situations.

Imprint- When humans imprint on something it means they decide to adopt ways of believing, functioning or solving life's dilemma. Childbearing women go through dramatic lifestyle changes, which requires a great deal of information they can choose to imprint on and eventually use. A good example if this is seen in a sharing support group where women watch each other care for their babies and choose to adopt techniques from each other. Another example is when a childbearing woman experiences some support that would fill in part of her own childhood development she can imprint on the experience and make it her own.

Introvert- Mary Sheedy Kurcinka, author of *Raising Your Spirited Child*, defines introverts as, "People who get their energy by being

alone with one or two special people. They prefer to interact with the world on the inside by reflecting on their thoughts and ideas before sharing them with others. They refresh themselves by spending time alone."[4]

Nurture- Loving, kind care that positively affects the well-being of the person who receives it. Clarke and Dawson define Nurture as, "All positive messages that encourage people to grow and thrive. Nurture helps people to love themselves and others."[5]

OK- A belief that who a person is is good, worth loving and deserve the goodness of life. When people believe they are OK they function in healthy ways, connect with others in helpful ways and find purpose in life. There are many things that contribute to a person's feeling of being OK, not least among them life experiences and the decisions one makes about who they are in those experiences.

Positive Strokes- A positive stroke is a message signaling to the receiver an affirming acceptance for her being alive and/or for what she does.

Recycle- The process of experiencing previous developmental stages with the skills gained from growing. Pam Levin defines it as "the process by which people re-experience earlier developmental stages in a more sophisticated manner at later stages." Jean Clarke discovered that parents will recycle the developmental stage of the child they are parenting triggered by the child. Recycling is a new opportunity to resolve any developmental task not fulfilled earlier in life."

Reframe- Human beings will put a "frame" on experiences in order to make sense of an experience. Frequently the frame is in the form of a feeling or belief about an experience or about oneself. Another way to define "frames" is the perception we carry in our memory of an experience. The "frame" may put the memory in a negative or positive light. Humans put "frames" on experiences in order to cope with the experience. When humans "reframe" an experience or a memory, they look at their perception and purposefully alter the "frame" they put on the experience. This evaluation process is done to offer a more helpful perception of life's experience. Another word for reframe is *rework*.

Rework- To rework a memory or a feeling is to consider the impact it has and to attempt to work toward remedying the impact or reframing. A goal of reworking a memory is to improve one's impression of an experience to shed any negative effects of the experience. By reworking a memory we improve ill effects it has caused. *Reframe* and *rework* are similar interchangeable terms.

Script Words- Words that a person adopts that play in their mind about their self-esteem and abilities.

Snapshot-like Memories- The memories that occur as a result of going through the childbearing year or any other life changing experience. Because the childbearing year is a time of important changes the events that take place can be firmly cemented forever set in your memory, almost like a photograph.[6]

Stroke- A stroke is a unit of recognition or human interaction. Strokes can be either negative or positive or both. Strokes like air, water and shelter are necessary for growth. All humans must receive strokes to survive, and they will take any kind of stroke available to them.[7]

Support Team- A group of people who agree to care for the childbearing woman in a way that she determined will be most helpful. These can be individuals of her family or individuals who are friends.

ENDNOTES

CHAPTER 1

1. This story is from Connie Dawson interview with the author, October 1995.

CHAPTER 2

1. Based on information from *Breastfeeding Success for Working Mothers* (Sheridan, WY: Achievement Press), by Marilyn Grams, M.D., by permission of the author.
2. Ibid.

CHAPTER 3

1. "You are an extravert/introvert if you . . ." from *Raising Your Spirited Child,* by Mary Sheedy Kurcinka, ©1991 by Mary Sheedy Kurcinka. Reprinted by permission of HarperCollins Publishers, Inc.

CHAPTER 4

1. This chapter is designed as a checklist—a garden plan. The emotional development steps of pregnancy were discovered by Reba Rubin, who is an expert in the "maternal tasks of pregnancy." She studied a large number of women and found that most of them seemed to experience the same type of developmental steps. *From Maternal Identity and the Maternal Experience* (New York: Springer Publishing Company, Inc.), by Reba Rubin, ©1984. Used by permission of the publisher.
2. Original design from *Growing Up Again: Parenting Ourselves, Parenting Our Children,* by Jean Illsley Clarke and Connie Dawson, ©1989 by Jean Illsley Clarke and Connie Dawson. Adapted by L. Kanyer and reprinted by permission of Hazelden Foundation, Center City, MN., pp. 58-59.
3. Ibid., pp. 58-59.
4. Ibid., p. 53.

CHAPTER 5

1. From "Just Another Day in a Woman's Life? Part II Nature and Consistency of Women's Long Term Perceptions of Their First Birth Experience," by Penny Simkin, PT, in *Birth* 19:2, June 1992. Used by permission of the author.

2. TA *for Tots, Powerful Techniques for Developing Self-Esteem* (Rolling Hills Estates, CA: Jalmar Press) 1973, by Alvyn and Margaret Freed, p. 20.

3. *The Yakama Time Ball, The Challenge of Spilyay,* The Yakama Nation, Yakama Nation Museum, Toppenish, WA, 1984, p. 4.

CHAPTER 6

1. Based on information from *The Newborn Mother: Steps of Her Growth,* by Andrea Boroff Eagan. ©1985 by Andrea Boroff Eagan. Reprinted by permission of Henry Holt and Co., Inc.

2. Adapted from *Growing Up Again: Parenting Ourselves, Parenting Our Children,* by Jean Illsley Clarke and Connie Dawson, ©1989 by Jean Illsley Clarke and Connie Dawson. Adapted by permission of Hazelden Foundation, Center City, MN, pp. 16-17.

3. Ibid., pp. 16-17.

4. Reprinted from *The Newborn Mother: Steps of Her Growth,* by Andrea Boroff Eagan, ©1985 by Andrea Boroff Eagan. Reprinted by permission of Henry Holt and Co., Inc.

5. Family Information Services, Minneapolis, MN. (800) 852-8112. From *Good Grief Rituals: Tools for Healing,* by Elaine Childs-Gowell, ©1992 by Elaine Childs-Gowell. Used by permission of Station Hill Press, Inc., p. 89.

CHAPTER 7

1. *Becoming the Way We Are: A Transactional Guide to Personal Development* (Berkeley, CA: Transactional Publications) ©1974 by Pamela Levin.

2. Excerpt from *Self-Esteem: A Family Affair,* by Jean Illsley Clarke, ©1981 by Jean Illsley Clarke. Reprinted by permission of the HarperCollins Publishers, p. 39.

3. Quoted from *Growing Up Again: Parenting Ourselves, Parenting Our Children,* by Jean Illsley Clarke and Connie Dawson, ©1989 by Jean Illsley Clarke and Connie Dawson. Reprinted by permission of Hazelden Foundation, Center City, MN, p. 111.

4. *Games People Play: The Psychology of Human Relationships.* (New York: Grove Press) 1964, by Eric Berne.

5. Quoted from *Growing Up Again: Parenting Ourselves, Parenting Our Children,* by Jean Illsley Clarke and Connie Dawson, ©1989 by Jean Illsley Clarke and Connie Dawson. Reprinted by permission of Hazelden Foundation, Center City, MN.

6. "Growing Up Again Clues and Activities," by Jean Illsley Clarke, in *We: A Newsletter for People Who Care About Self-Esteem* 9:3 (May-June 1990). Used by permission of the author.

7. Quoted from *Growing Up Again: Parenting Ourselves, Parenting Our Children,* by Jean Illsley Clarke and Connie Dawson, ©1989 by Jean Illsley Clarke and Connie Dawson. Reprinted by permission of Hazelden Foundation, Center City, MN, p. 162

CHAPTER 8

1. Adapted from *Pick Up Your Socks: A Practical Guide to Raising Responsible Children,* by Elizabeth Crary, ©1990 by Elizabeth Crary, pp. 76-77, and *Growing Up Again: Parenting Ourselves, Parenting Our Children,* by Jean Illsley Clarke and Connie Dawson, ©1989 by

Jean Illsley Clarke and Connie Dawson. Adapted by permission of Hazelden Foundation, Center City, MN, pp. 150-151.

2. Adapted from *Growing Up Again: Parenting Ourselves, Parenting Our Children,* by Jean Illsley Clarke and Connie Dawson, ©1989 by Jean Illsley Clarke and Connie Dawson. Adapted by permission of Hazelden Foundation, Center City, MN, p. 162.

3. Ibid., p. 143.

4. Adapted from *The Blessing,* by Gary Smalley and John Trent (Nashville, TN: Thomas Nelson Publishers, 1986). Adapted by permission of the publisher.

5. Ibid.

CHAPTER 9

1. Adapted from *Growing Up Again: Parenting Ourselves, Parenting Our Children,* by Jean Illsley Clarke and Connie Dawson, ©1989 by Jean Illsley Clarke and Connie Dawson. Adapted by permission of Hazelden Foundation, Center City, MN, p. 168.

CHAPTER 10

1. From *Self-Esteem: A Family Affair Leader's Guide* by Jean Illsley Clarke, ©1978 by Jean Illsley Calrke (San Franciso, CA: HarperCollins Publishers, Inc. Used by permission of the author, p, 37.

2. Adapted from *Growing Up Again: Helping Ourselves, Helping Our Children, Six-Week Parenting Course Curriculum* by Jean Illsley Clarke, ©1989 by Jean Illsley Clarke. Adapted by permission of Hazelden Foundation, Center City, MN, p. 7.

3. Ibid., p. 3.

TERMS USED IN THE BOOK

1. Quoted from *Self-Esteem: A Family Affair* by Jean Illsley Clarke, ©1978 by Jean Illsley Calrke (Minneapolis, MN: Winston Press, Inc.). Used by permission of the publisher, p, 263.

2. Quoted from *Growing Up Again: Parenting Ourselves, Parenting Our Children,* by Jean Illsley Clarke and Connie Dawson, ©1989 by Jean Illsley Clarke and Connie Dawson. Used by permission of Hazelden Foundation, Center City, MN, p. 109.

3. Quoted from *Raising Your Spirited Child,* by Mary Sheedy Kurcinka, ©1992 by Mary Sheedy Kurcinka. Reprinted by permission of HarperCollins Publishers, Inc., p. 53.

4. Ibid., p. 53.

5. Quoted from *Growing Up Again: Parenting Ourselves, Parenting Our Children,* by Jean Illsley Clarke and Connie Dawson, ©1989 by Jean Illsley Clarke and Connie Dawson. Used by permission of Hazelden Foundation, Center City, MN, p. 6.

6. Adapted from "Just Another Day in a Woman's Life? Part II Women's Long-Term Perceptions of Their First Birth Experience," by Penny Simkin, in *Birth* 18:4 (December 1991).

7. Quoted from *Self-Esteem: A Family Affair,* by Jean Illsley Clarke, ©1978 by Jean Illsley Clarke (Minneapolis, MN: Winston Press, Inc.). Used by permission of the publisher, p. 273.

BIBLIOGRAPHY

Bardsley, Sandra, and Lucia Capacchione. *Creating a Joyful Birth Experience: Developing a Partnership With Your Unborn Child for Healthy Pregnancy, Labor, and Early Parenting.* New York: Simon & Schuster, 1994.

Bass, Ellen, and Laura Davis. *The Courage to Heal: A Guide for Women Survivors of Child Sexual Abuse.* New York: HarperCollins Publishers, Inc., 1992.

Berends, Polly Berrien. *Whole Child/Whole Parent.* New York: Harper & Row Publishers, 1983.

Berne, Eric. *Games People Play: The Psychology of Human Relationships.* New York: Grove Press, 1964.

Brazelton, T. Berry. *Touchpoints: Your Child's Emotional and Behavioral Development.* Reading, MA: Addison Wesley Publishing, 1992.

Buzan, Tony. *Use Both Sides of Your Brain.* New York: E.P. Dutton, 1983.

Carlson, Karin. *Infant Feeding Program Survey.* Yakima, WA: Yakima Valley Memorial Hospital, 1995.

Childs-Gowell, Elaine. *Good Grief Rituals: Tools for Healing.* Barrytown, NY: Station Hill Press, 1992.

Clarke, Jean Illsley. "Growing Up Again Clues and Activities." *We: A Newsletter for People Who Care About Self-Esteem* 9 (3): May-June 1990.

———— *Growing Up Again: Helping Ourselves, Helping Our Children Six-Week Parenting Course Curriculum.* Unpublished work.

———— *Self-Esteem: A Family Affair.* Minneapolis, MN: Winston Press, Inc., 1978.

———— *Self-Esteem: A Family Affair Leader's Guide.* San Francisco, CA: HarperCollins Publishers, Inc., 1978.

———— *Who Me, Lead a Group?* New York: HarperCollins Publishers, Inc., 1984.

Clarke, Jean Illsley, and Connie Dawson. *Growing Up Again: Parenting Ourselves, Parenting Our Children.* New York: Hazelden Books/Harper Collins Publishers, 1989.

Crary, Elizabeth. *Pick Up Your Socks: A Practical Guide to Raising Responsible Children.* Seattle, WA: Parenting Press, 1980.

Eagan, Andrea Boroff. *The Newborn Mother: Stages of Her Growth.* Boston: Little, Brown & Company, 1985.

Faber, Adele, and Elaine Mazlish. *Liberated Parents, Liberated Children.* New York: Avon Books, 1974.

Family Information Services Professional Resource Materials. Minneapolis, MN: Family Information Services, 1994.

Freed, Alvyn, and Margaret Freed. *TA for Tots: Powerful Techniques for Developing Self-Esteem.* Rolling Hills Estates, CA: Jalmar Press, 1973.

Galinsky, Ellen. *Between Generations: The Six Stages of Parenthood.* New York: Addison Wesley Publishing, 1987.

Gesme, Carol, and Russ Osnes. *TA 101 Training*. Central Regional Prenatal Program. Yakima, WA: Yakima Valley Memorial Hospital, 1994.

Grams, Marilyn. *Breastfeeding Success for Working Mothers*. Sheridan, WY: Achievement Press, 1985.

Jones, Sandy. *Crying Babies, Sleepless Nights*. Boston: Harvard Common Press, 1992.

Klaus, Marshall H., John Kennel, and Phyllis Klaus. *Mother the Mother: How a Doula Can Help You Have a Shorter, Easier, and Healthier Birth*. New York: Addison Wesley Publishing, 1993.

Kirkham, Maura A. *Reducing Stress in Mothers of Children With Special Needs*. Seattle, WA: University of Washington Press, 1988.

Kurcinka, Mary Sheedy. *Raising Your Spirited Child: A Guide for Parents Whose Child is More Intense, Sensitive, Perceptive, Persistent . . .* New York: HarperCollins Publishers, Inc., 1991.

Levin, Pamela. *Becoming the Way We Are: A Transactional Guide to Personal Development*. Berkeley, CA: Transactional Publications, 1974.

Motherhood: A Keepsake Book With Quotes. Philadalphia: Running Press Book Publishers, 1990.

Paananen, Mary. *Growing Up Again Facilitator's Training*. Central Washington Regional Perinatal Program. Yakima, WA: Yakima Valley Memorial Hospital, 1993.

Pessel, Molly. *Breastfeeding Basics Training*. Kirkland, WA: Evergreen Hospital, 1993.

Piersa, Eileen. "Effects of Different Approaches of Goal Setting on Goal Commitment." Masters Thesis, Organizational Development. Ellensburg, WA: Central Washington University, 1990.

Placksin, Sally. *Mothering the New Mother: Your Postpartum Resource Companion*. New York: Newmarket Press, 1994.

Rhode, Naomi. *The Gift of Family: A Legacy of Love*. Nashville, TN: Thomas Nelson Publishers, 1991.

Rico, Gabriele Lusser. *Writing the Natural Way: Using Right Brain Techniques to Release Your Expressive Powers*. New York: St. Martin's Press, 1983.

Rubin, Reva. *Maternal Identity and the Maternal Experience*. New York: Springer Publishing Company, 1984.

Saavedra, Beth Wilson. *Meditaitons for New Mothers*. New York: Workman Publishing, 1992.

St. James, Elaine. *Simplify Your Life: 100 Ways to Slow Down and Enjoy the Things That Really Matter*. New York: Hyperion, 1994.

Samuels, Michael, Nancy Samuels, and Wendy Frost. *The Well Child Book*. New York: Summit Books, 1982.

Sark. *Inspiration Sandwich*. Berkeley, CA: Celestial Arts, 1992.

Sears, Martha and William Sears. *The Baby Book: Everything You Need to Know About Your Baby From Birth to Age Two*. Boston: Little, Brown and Company, 1993.

Simkin, Penny. *Just Another Day in a Woman's Life? Part I: Women's Long-Term Perceptions of Their First Birth Experience*. Birth 18:4, December 1991.

——— *Just Another Day in a Woman's Life? Part II: Nature and Consistency of Women's Long-Term Perceptions of Their First Birth Experience*. Birth 19:2, June 1992.

Simkin, Penny, Janet Whalley, and Ann Keppler. *Pregnancy, Childbirth and the Newborn*. New York: Meadowbrook Press, 1991.

Smalley, Gary, and John Trent. *The Blessing*. Nashville, TN: Thomas Nelson Publishers, 1986.

Stinnet, Nick, and John DeFrain. *Secrets of Strong Families*. Boston: Little, Brown and Company, 1985.

Stoddard, Alexandra. *Living a Beautiful Life: Five Hundred Ways to Add Elegance, Order, Beauty, and Joy to Every Day of Your Life*. New York: Random House, 1986.

Winnicott, D.W. *Babies and Their Mothers*. Reading, MA: Addison Wesley Publishing, 1987.

Yakama Indian Nation. *The Yakama Time Ball: The Challenge of Spilyay*. Toppenish, WA: Yakama Nation Museum, 1984.

INDEX